to Francis, w[illegible] so much joy and satisfaction to Phil over the years. Thanks you for continuing to respond to "Come sit beside me on the piano (organ) bench - listen to me, hurt with me, rejoice with me, learn with me, laugh with me, at me and for me."

Sincerely,

Goldie and Alvin

COME AND SEE

COME AND SEE

Ken Medema
with Joyce Norman

WORD BOOKS, PUBLISHER
WACO, TEXAS

To my wife,

JANE

*Who is my poetry, my full
moon, my summer breeze and
snow-covered winter morning.*

And to my son,

LEE AARON

*Who I pray will become a
finer Christian and a better
man than his father.*

Contents

Foreword

I answered my phone, and the voice on the other end said, "Kurt, I would never bother you at home, but there's this blind pianist-singer who has been performing at Baylor University for the Women's Missionary Union Annual Convention. You must hear him!" The caller was an excellent singer and friend, Ron Owens. Any singer Ron recommended, I wanted to hear!

The next morning, into my office came Ken and Jane Medema and Ron and Patricia Owens. Through the years, I've heard many people sing and many people play, but I anticipated this morning with genuine excitement.

I'll never forget how moved I became as Ken played and sang, "Stop right here, there's a Fork in the Road." I remember tears. This man knew what he was doing; he'd gone to school, that was obvious. He also wrote in extended forms—not the usual 16 or 32 measure song. I then rounded up several other people to see their reaction to this incisive, sensitive, musician. Their reaction was the same as mine.

Ken Medema, through the several years that we've had association, has maintained a high level of creativity in his writing. I've often felt that when he has completed his preachment through music, no other word need be spoken.

9

COME AND SEE

Ken continues to grow as a Christian witness and actively pursues study which enriches his personal pilgrimage, and then, so beautifully, the pilgrimage of all of us who hear him.

KURT KAISER

Preface

This is not a book that would be titled "The Ken Medema Story." You'll find no near-death, traumatic catastrophies in the following pages. Nor have I struggled against tremendous odds. There's no prison story.

Your story is probably as interesting as mine. My only reason for writing this book is that you may be able to identify with me through some of my experiences and sharing.

Perhaps it will affirm some of the things you may have been doubting. Maybe my being honest with you will spark new beginnings of honesty within yourself.

Do not sit in awe at the "poor limited blind child," but, rather, when you read my story, retell your own.

Acknowledgments

My thanks to Joyce who has prodded, nudged, encouraged and bugged me, and who gave me the opportunity that few people are afforded to open the windows of the past and to explore the meaning of the present.

It would be a special pleasure to work with you again, Joyce Norman. I like the way your heart and head come together—even in the morning.

I wish to thank Alice Wisdom for a beautiful job of typing the first draft of the manuscript.

I wish also to thank my editors at Word Books, Floyd Thatcher, executive editor, Margaret Walding, editor, and Ken Clark, copy editor, for their helpful suggestions and editorial guidance.

KEN MEDEMA

1

First Notes

The temperature was ten below zero that winter day in the Michigan State University football stadium. Other than the howling wind there wasn't a sound to be heard anywhere. This was an unusual day, an unusual time, and a most unusual game. The day—December, after football season. The time—my first semester at MSU on my way to class. The game—a blind guy fighting the panic of being swallowed up by this huge man-made crater. The score is zero for the lonely fellow who doesn't wish to play this game at all.

The football stadium at MSU is a big place when you're sitting in the stands on a Saturday afternoon surrounded by thousands of enthusiastic, loud students. That same stadium is even larger when you can't see; when you've accidentally taken the wrong sidewalk and unknowingly walked through a gate that has been left open and wandered onto the enormous field. And there's not a soul anywhere in sound.

I cannot describe the awful sinking feeling I had: Nobody will find me. What will I do? Alone, afraid,

15

I was lost—lost in the confines of a football stadium. It was a scary place. I had been in that stadium many times, but someone had always been there cleaning, repairing, running the office. On this very cold winter day there was no one. It seemed that I wandered around that field forever trying to find a way out.

This incident and others like it form only a part of my story. It's not all that dramatic or colorful. Much of it is plain, ordinary living.

I'd like for you to join me while I tell my story. I admit I'm not a writer and putting together a book scares me a bit. So, I'm going to tell you my story in the way that is most comfortable for me—singing and playing it to you.

I'd like for you to sit with me on the piano bench as I sing some of my songs. There will probably be places where you'll want to sing along because my song is so much like yours. There will be sections where my music will differ from yours a good deal. That's all right for your song is important, too, and you need to experience the joy of singing it.

Everything is quiet in our music hall and I begin to play the first notes of the evening. As the piano keys respond to my fingers and music begins to rise from that magnificent instrument, I recall the hundreds of times I have sat down to play those first notes.

I remember the anticipation and perspiration of a 100-degree night in Cleveland, Ohio, in 1972, when I sang for a Billy Graham Crusade.

I shudder with fear when I remember my first music-making session with a group of indifferent teenagers in a psychiatric hospital in New Jersey. I was a music therapist. My job was to love them, teach them, encourage them to express themselves, help them find new skills, and eventually, new freedom. They did not care at all. They weren't interested!

I remember my confidence on senior recital day. After warming up in the morning, spending the afternoon in bed, indulging in a huge steak and a glass of orange juice, I walked out on stage to play what I knew would be a fine program.

My first day in a recording studio was full of uneasiness. The tape was rolling. The pros were there. Hundreds of dollars were being spent and I was sure I would blow it any minute. In fact, I did blow it—several times. They did, too, so I felt better.

I have never been so close to being in orbit as I was the day I first played with a jazz group. "O.K., Medema, you've got it. Take a ride." I knew the stage was mine. The rhythm was backing me up and I took off all over the keyboard. Clumsily? Yes. Trying too hard to impress. As we went along there was a rapport between us that is hardly equaled in any other form of music-making.

As a junior in high school I played my first notes with an orchestra. I had been chosen piano soloist with the Grand Rapids Michigan Youth Symphony. My inner voice said to me, as I walked to the keyboard amid the applause, "What if the conductor doesn't like my tempo? What if I forget how long the orchestra interludes are?" I later came to the conclusion that either the conductor did like my tempo or I simply couldn't see his attempts to change it. Either way, we all finished at the same place.

I felt a tremendous sense of power when I played my first chords on the pipe organ at church. There I was, controlling all that air pressure with those hundreds of pipes making all that sound. It seemed almost too good to be true!

My earliest recollections of playing first notes bring me back to the age of seven. There was an old upright piano in the living room of my parents' home on the west side of Grand Rapids. As I became familiar with the instrument I graduated from one-finger melodies to playing chords with three fingers on the right hand. My father was not a musician but he had some very practical advice: "Son, you have a thumb. Use it."

My first formal study was with an elderly gentleman who had a studio in downtown Grand Rapids. I believe I was eight at the time. He introduced me to Braille music. He cautioned me weekly about the dangers of playing too much by ear and not relying on the score. When I was ten or eleven years old he died. After several months of searching I began studying with Miss Heather Halstead. I must tell you more about Heather in a moment, but for now it is enough to say that she contributed more to my musical training than all the other teachers, performers, and heroes in my life. She baked the cake. They put on the icing.

It seemed there was always some kind of music-making in my life and wherever the music was I found a place to belong and to excel. Today I am most comfortable in social situations or when meeting strangers if such meetings focus around music. That's not unusual, I suppose. Each one of us carries his or her own security blanket into everyday life. Some of us rely on the fact that we are good "get-acquainters." Some of us depend on the comments that might be made about our good looks. Some of us have a conversational style or a kind of humor which sets us apart and makes us special. There have been many occasions when I have felt uncomfortable and unable to function smoothly because of not being able to see what is happening around me. But such occasions are eased when music is a part of the situation.

Musical opportunities were abundant when I was a child. I sang in the children's choir at church, and at ten I was boy soprano soloist with the adult choir. I accompanied all the singing for my class in primary school; played the part of "chief cherub" in some Christmas programs; and felt immensely smug when accompanying the singing of the national anthem for school assemblies.

Whenever family and friends would come to visit in the evenings I was always called on to play a piece or two before being shuffled off to bed. When those mini-recitals were over I would stand just beyond the upstairs door for a few minutes to see what the grownups would say about my performance. If somebody caught me there it was always possible to go up to my room and listen through the heat register. Sound carried through it from the living room directly to my bedroom. The only problem was that when they talked about my performance they talked in such hushed tones it was difficult to hear.

The adjustments to junior high and high school were made much easier because I almost immediately became involved in the music program. I remember the sense of security I felt each day when I walked into the choral room at Grand Rapids Christian High School. When those doors closed behind me I knew that for the next hour I would be in my element, totally at home. No place is as satisfying as the place where you know you belong.

Now, let me talk about Miss Heather Halstead for a moment. I suppose if I were to list the ten most influential people in my life Heather would figure prominently on that list. From the first day she made the study of music an exciting adventure. She introduced me to much of what I now know of the history and theory of music.

Every lesson was a treasure hunt. We sought not only to learn to play a piece, but to discover what makes music tick and why composers do what they do. We listened to all kinds of music. The most important element in all of this was that Heather cared deeply about her students.

Heather received her training at Curtis Institute of Music in Philadelphia and Juilliard School of Music in New York. She had no family of her own so her pupils became a kind of family. In addition to lessons we came together often as a group to talk about music, listen to each other perform, and just have fun.

Later, when I went to study music at Michigan State University, I was continually surprised to find that much of my college music curriculum consisted of material I had already learned. You can imagine the tremendous advantage this gave me. But on the other hand it sometimes tended to make me a rather lazy student.

Besides being a fine teacher and an excellent musician, Heather was a lover of literature and history. Her caring for us as pupils and as persons led her to introduce us to great books. My first contact with Socrates was in her music studio. She read to me from books by everyone from Gilbert Hyatt to Alfred North Whitehead to Plato.

It became obvious to me that Heather was not at all comfortable with the religious tradition in which I was growing up. She was not a Christian as I now know a Christian to be. I am not willing to say she was unrelated to God but she certainly had departed from conservative Christianity.

We began to speak of religion and I found myself very receptive to anything she might say. My desire to please her led me to ask questions about my church background, about the existence of God and about, what seemed at the time, the narrow and limited beliefs of my parents. By the time I was a junior in high school I was a self-proclaimed rebel and my inner voice was screaming to get away from Calvinist tradition.

Heather exposed me to the sermons of Dr. Duncan Littlefair, the pastor of Fountain Street Church in my hometown. Fountain Street proclaimed itself to be a liberal church and I found in that community a comfortable place from which to militate against what I thought were the chains and fetters of my Christian Reformed past.

I don't know if my parents were aware of what was happening to me. They must have known something because a great deal of tension began to arise between us. My loyalties were definitely committed to my new friends and nothing that home or church told me could change that. The conflict came to a head when I resisted my parents' desire to send me to Calvin College. I was determined instead to go to a state university.

Looking back on that period of time reminds me of the excitement of audition day—the feeling of confidence when I sat down at the keyboard before those university professors to play the music I had worked on so long and the tremendous exhilaration I felt when I was accepted into music school.

"Heather, you must have been proud, too. You never said it, but you must have felt all your work and time were worthwhile. You taught me more than music. You taught me that asking questions was part of being human. You taught me that a teacher can truly care about the welfare of students. You opened the door for me to literature and philosophy. You gave me confidence in myself and in my strengths, and you, more than anyone before or after you, made me truly want to learn and grow."

Those first notes are about to give way to a song. But before they do I wish to express my thanks to a singer, a very special singer—Mrs. Trina Haan. She was the director of the choral music program at Grand Rapids Christian High School. She was held in high regard by choral directors all over the state. Her choirs were always first-rate. She knew how to produce good singers. She not only gave me a foundation of knowledge about singing, but she kindly, gently took my ego down a notch or two when it needed to be taken down. She showed me what it was to be a part of a highly disciplined performance group. That learning has had tremendous effects on my practice of music therapy. I discovered when people work together in a group to perform to the best of their ability, they can achieve a unity of purpose and an awareness of each other's needs that bring about a lot of good therapy for everyone involved.

My first notes have set the style for the evening. In those notes we find questioning, challenge, ambivalence, discovery, excitement and hope. Now it's time for the song to begin.

2

~~~~~~~~~~~~~~ *Symphony of Praise*

The sun on my face in the morning,
Birds' wings beating in the sky,
Somewhere in the quiet of the first light
I can hear a newborn baby cry.

I wrote this song for my son, Aaron, and every time
I sing it, as I'm doing now, I think of him.

But tonight I'm also thinking of my mother, especially when I hear the last part of the first stanza:

Somewhere in the quiet of the first light
I can hear a newborn baby cry.

The baby's cry? Oh, yes, my mother remembers the first cry I made and perhaps after this song I'll play an interlude and let her talk to you about those days. She's very capable at analyzing her feelings. She's neat!

The touch of sand on my running feet,
The ocean roaring nearby,
Above the sound of the surf and the seagulls
I still can hear the newborn's cry.

How well I remember those "little boy" days when I'd run as fast as I could along the beaches of Lake Michigan. I guess I was in search of an experience of real free flight. Most of my dreams as a youngster were about flying and I suppose that's why one of my most-often used songs is, *Come with Me, Fly with Me.*

I always thought flying was the greatest thing, and the next best thing to flying was running in the sand on the Lake Michigan beaches. I remember that there was nothing but long stretches of beach for miles and miles. What a joy! What an exhilarating experience it was to run so fast and actually feel my feet leave the sand for a few seconds and "fly!"

I must add here, though, that I had some pretty exciting "flying" times on my bicycle. All fantasy, but all tremendously fun. I would ride around and around our block and most of the time I'd pretend I was the pilot of a great airplane. Sometimes my bike would be a police car or a race car, but it was always something that moved fast. Mostly, my bike was a high-flying plane.

On vacations and weekends, my parents, my younger sister, Mary, and I would go camping near the lake. I'd often get up very early in the mornings and leave the camp where we had our trailer or tent. We never owned our own camping gear but borrowing it was just as good.

Anyway, I'd leave the camp and I would run, run, run, run, run down the beach. I'd run very near the

25

lake so that I could swim awhile and then get up and run fast again.

It was a big lake and there were high waves most of the time. What fun—running hard on the sandy beach, splashing in the water and getting knocked down by a wave, digging in the sand (all right, I *did* throw some sand occasionally!). Can you imagine the abandon!

I had a favorite spot, too—Silver Lake, Michigan. Silver Lake feeds into Lake Michigan through a long channel. Along the sides of the channel are steep sand dunes. I would climb up on a sand dune, lie down perpendicular to the hill, and *roll* and *roll* and *roll* down the hill until I'd roll smack into the water. There was nothing to stop me.

For me, that rolling was the ultimate let go. But, I soon discovered another kind of freedom that brought pure ecstasy to me. When I was ten years old my Uncle Fred taught me to water ski!

My uncle had a cottage near White Fish Lake, a small inland lake in Michigan. He had a boat and he knew how much I loved everything about water, so he taught me to ski.

How well I remember the feeling of getting up on those skis and gliding behind that boat. It was the greatest feeling to know I had that whole expanse of water and that I couldn't run into anything! This was like a third dimension for me. It was the closest thing to flying I'd found.

When the day came that I read *Jonathan Livingston*

Seagull, I discovered I had a kinship with that bird. I still dream of being in flight to this day.

I remember some interesting dynamics about those family outings to the beach. My dad would come home from a long week of work and would like nothing better than to stay home on Saturday and watch a football game, cut the grass or maybe just take it easy.

Mom, on the other hand, had had a long week with Mary and me hanging around the house. Maybe she would have liked to spend some time with dad. But, they took us out. I believe they felt an obligation-need to provide recreation for us that other kids found for themselves.

I enjoyed playing alone sometimes and one of my favorite activities was playing with scraps of ceramic tile. Dad brought home all shapes and sizes of tile for me and with them I built houses, garages, hotels, and places for my boats and cars. On the front porch of my home I created all those magnificent structures.

I suppose I enjoyed the tiles so much because there weren't many books to read and I didn't have many friends. There weren't, at least for me, puzzles to work or comics to read. There was television but that wasn't always very interesting.

When tiles, television, bicycling, and all else failed, we raised the standard cry of the twentieth-century American child, "Mom, what can I do?" Mom and dad would find things to do and sacrifice their own pleasure to do *with* us.

Thinking back to the sand dunes, I remember a funny incident that took place there years after I was a youngster. I had met Jane, who was to become my wife, and I wanted to take her back to my old stomping grounds, so we went to the sand dunes near Silver Lake. There is some very high reed grass up on those dunes. One can pick it, hold it just right in the wind and it will vibrate—buzzzzz. There we were—gregarious father, sedate mother, Mary with long hair trailing in the wind, enthusiastic Ken, and uncertain Jane buzzing reed grass when the stranger's question came, "Excuse me, what religious sect is this?"

Another important part of my freedom was my friend, Jerry. We did everything together—especially we dreamed together. Sprawled out across my bed we dreamed into existence great estates, magnificent river boats, elaborate churches, and the world's greatest pipe organs. Actually, *I* built the pipe organs; *he* built other things.

I remember one of the most delightful parts of our friendship was borrowing my mom's old 1950 Chevrolet. Jerry was sixteen, and a junior in high school, and I was seventeen, and a senior. We went to the beach, to the dunes or to the woods. Sometimes we would take a lunch to the woods, but wherever we went, we were always having fun.

I'm glad Jerry decided to major in music therapy. I think he did so primarily because of having seen it work for me. Jerry probably wouldn't have been in music at all had we not gotten together. So you see, it was a good friendship—we helped each other.

Jerry and I double-dated a lot in high school and my only problem was that I was interested both in my girl and in his girl, too. I suppose I will always resent the fact that I seldom dated the girls who were the objects of my fondest fantasies. I was grateful for any female attention, but like most guys, my heart was set on those who were reserved for the basketball heroes and college boys.

The third verse of this song I'm singing is:

> The sun on my face in the morning,
> The gentle sound of springtime rain.

I love to listen to rain! I love to listen to all sorts of sounds. I remember as a child lying on the floor with my ear next to the refrigerator so I could hear its motor humming. Even that cast on my foot brought rhythmic sounds as I recall banging against objects with it. I've always loved sounds. Maybe sounds are special because that's one of the ways I "see" this world.

> The touch of a hand on my shoulder,
> Gentle sleep to ease my pain.

Yes, there was some of that. I suppose I must tell you that I don't like to make a big thing out of pain. It would be very easy in a book like this to emphasize the times that were painful. Perhaps you can see the picture of the poor, unhappy, unfortunate blind child who has been excluded from all of life's best experiences, yet with a determination and a smile on his face, says bravely, courageously, "I shall live."

It wasn't exactly that way. Sometimes I did feel like a rather insignificant person. I remember very well the times I spent on the playground at the junior high school listening to the boys kick a football, tossing a basketball and enjoying other sports. Why not me?

In the ninth grade I had a crush on Sara Smith but she was interested in Lynn Schrader who was one of the athletic, self-confident fellows who always made baskets and kicked the ball just right. I wanted to do it, too, because I thought maybe Sara would look at me. As it was, Lynn was better-looking at the time, and maybe more grown up. Maybe he even had more peach fuzz than I did. No matter, for Sara liked Lynn and I liked Sara.

I can also recall the nobody feeling when as a high school junior I would sometimes walk around the block at lunchtime, usually alone, while others walked hand in hand or (even worse) drove around in their cars. I was the only sixteen-year-old in the school who had to say to a girl, "My mother and I will pick you up for the concert."

I also remember walking down the halls at school wishing certain people would notice me or that I could point them out or find them. I recall being so comfortable in the music activities and so uncomfortable in other places. I especially remember wishing that I could see and be just like everybody else.

This feeling didn't last much after high school. You change, I suppose. But there was pain. There was pain in elementary school when I had to go into the special class for the blind and couldn't go into the regular class. The kids in the regular class seemed so neat. Kids in the Braille class seemed so dull.

I suppose my little sister had more pain than I. I was always "the brilliant, young musician." Mary was always somewhat in the back seat. She has spoken to me of her pain about this. Her childhood years, especially in junior and senior high school, were rather uncomfortable. Part of that, I suppose, had to do with the fact that mom, dad, and I tended to put Mary in a back seat role. I know now that when she withdrew to her room to do her artwork, straining her eyes to see detail, shaping the clay to perfection over and over again, she was bearing that pain.

But I'm happy for Mary now. She is married to Steve Barber and lives in Des Moines, Iowa. Presently, she is teaching blind children in Smouse Opportunities School.

However, you must not think that I went through these huge paroxysms of grief and pain. No, life was not a miserable experience for me. Life for me was really quite good. There were moments of hurt, maybe more than some other kids had, and I did feel like a nobody a lot of the time. I wanted desperately for people to like me—especially the girls!

31

Oh yes, there was some physical discomfort involved and I have a permanent bruise on my forehead to remind me of the times I've run into clotheslines, lampposts, sides of buildings and other "small" objects.

As a teenager I used to really try to act cool when I'd run into something. You know the role: Mr. Very Cool. Ignore it. Don't let anybody know. Straighten up right away. Quick recovery of lost composure.

I can recall many times walking head-long into a signpost or some other object and immediately backing up, turning and walking on down the street and whistling a little louder as if to say, "See that neat thing I just did? Well, I meant to do that."

So, my song ends:

> These are the songs, my son.
> Raise your voice and sing, my son.
> Join in the Symphony of Praise.

These are some of the things I remember in the search during those early years for the freedom to move and change and grow and act and run.

Now comes the interlude and my mom will share with you.

3

Somewhere in the quiet of the first light
I can hear a newborn baby cry.

"Along with the tears of a newborn baby were the
tears of a mother when she found out her newborn
baby had a very severe clubfoot. We brought Ken
home from the hospital with a cast on his right foot.
That was pretty hard for a twenty-two-year-old
mother to cope with. My husband Hank and I didn't
know it at the time, but we were to see that cast on
Ken's foot for two years.

"The first year, monthly, it was taken off and the
next day the doctor would put on another one. I vividly
remember those days when the cast was off because
we furiously took pictures! Every picture you see of
Ken as a baby is without his cast because we took
them that one day when the cast was removed. The
excitement of dressing him up in those cute little short
pants and not having that awful thing on his foot was
the impetus for taking our son to visit friends and

family. It didn't seem to matter that one leg was thinner than the other. It was so exciting and I lived for those times when the cast was taken off for just one day.

"After a year Ken had to go to the hospital overnight because he had to be anesthetized. At this point there was much more pain involved. The doctors had to manipulate the foot, twisting and turning it to make it as straight as possible. Then, another cast was put on. This hospital ordeal was a traumatic experience for most of the time my husband was not with me. Hank had been in the navy since Ken was four months old so Ken's Grandpa Medema went with us. Ken had minor surgery on his foot twice before he was five years old. When he was eight, he had major surgery. At this time the doctors were able to form his foot so that he could walk without so distinctive a limp.

"The cast at that time seemed great. However, it wasn't great when we look back and recall our discovery that after six weeks when babies should be following movements and looking at things, Ken was not. The monthly trips to the pediatrician for the regular shots and examinations and checkups always yielded the same answer, 'It's too early to tell. Wait another month and we'll see what happens. Perhaps he's just slow.'

"We told ourselves these things until Ken was three months old and then the realization and final recognition forced us to admit the awful truth I had been afraid to think of. The moment of truth occurred the day my sister came for a visit. She had not seen Ken before and when she looked at him in his crib she quickly looked up at me and said, 'But Marion, the baby does not see me!'

"This was the 'letting go' time. The outburst of tears, the coming-apart-at-the-seams, the accepting and admitting to ourselves the stark knowledge that Ken was blind.

"At four months he was taken to an eye surgeon who seemed to play the same tune for us, 'I can't tell you anything. Ken is too young.' I recall that this doctor was a very blunt man. How well I remember him saying, 'He's too young to really tell but I don't think your baby will ever have vision.' I think I despise that man to this day for telling me so bluntly that Ken would never see.

"Our pediatrician kept a close check on him and after six months told me, 'Perhaps you ought to go to Ann Arbor, Michigan, for further tests.' Hank came home on leave and we took Ken to Ann Arbor. Again we were told that it was too soon for tests to determine what was wrong with him. The doctors did tell us, though, that he was an unusually healthy baby. They took x-rays of his brain and made extensive tests, but they felt there was no then-known operation that would help him. Yet, they told us, 'Perhaps it's still too early to tell for sure. Come back in a year.'

"A year later, however, they confirmed the fact that Ken had congenital searching nystagmus and there was nothing they could do for him. In layman's terms, Ken's eyes are perfectly formed, but there is no connection

35

from the optic nerve to the brain. There is a searching and a movement of the eyes and he cannot focus at all.

"After Ken had been to Ann Arbor for the second time (he was about one-and-a-half years old) he was seen periodically by Dr. R. H. Gilbert, the eye surgeon who saw him up to the time he left high school. But Dr. Gilbert's examinations were only to check and be sure nothing more had developed. By this time, we knew for sure that Ken would never see.

"My husband and I went to classes with other parents of blind children. These classes were a great source of help because of the problems unique to parents of blind children. The interaction of the group and exchange of ideas allowed us to draw strength from one another.

"We were encouraged to bring up Ken to the best of our ability as if he were a normal child. As far as we knew, Ken never wished he could see nor did he seem to miss doing many of the things the other kids did. That's why we were quite surprised to hear him express these feelings later on in life. We *never* knew Ken was despondent. We *never* knew he had any 'whys?' We feel all this stems from the fact that we never allowed pity in the house. Ken was treated in most ways like a normal child.

"Of course, there were certain things that were different out of necessity. For example, most of my friends were able to move their living room furniture around occasionally. This sticks in my mind, I guess, because I have a friend who moves her furniture weekly. That was something we could not do. We had to *think* and *plan* things relative to Ken's handicap.

"Ken was three years old when Hank and I knew we were going to have another baby. I don't remember having much discomfort at the time I was carrying the second baby. I never worried about the child being born blind and never had thoughts of having anything but a healthy baby. We felt whatever the Lord had planned was right. The doctor mentioned nothing about heredity. He simply told us that with Ken the connections from the optic nerve to the brain were nonexistent. He never told us we *could* have another blind child. Of course, my strength and optimistic attitude, I know, came from God. I was not concerned about the new baby, only excited.

"You see, I had worried so about Ken, watching him learn to crawl, and I wondered how he would ever walk. The time came when he walked the way most babies do. I was glad to have that hurdle behind me.

"Then I wondered how he would play out of doors, and by the time he was two and a half and walking beautifully the out of doors had become his territory. Slowly, we began to realize that God was behind us and helping us. These experiences had drawn us not only closer to each other, but had drawn us closer to God. We were aware there had to be Someone behind us showing us the way.

"By the time our baby girl, Mary, was born I was in high spirits. The first six weeks were traumatic, I remember, because there was that constant watching over her, looking to see when she was going to follow movement. Mary did show us some following in her eyes and we felt relieved. You must understand that even the smallest eye movement was the greatest hope for Hank and me!

"There were the routine trips to the doctor but by three months we were told Mary was blind, although she had a better degree of vision than Ken. (Ken is able in bright sunlight to make out buildings, trees, cars and other large objects but there is never any detail, just forms. When it is cloudy or nearing dusk, he sees only darkness.)

"As you might imagine, this was a very difficult thing for us. In fact, it was so hard I came very close to leaving my own faith and seeking help from Christian Science. I had a sister (the very same sister who made us realize that Ken was blind) who said, 'I can help you. Ken can see. You take him to a Christian Science practitioner (a person who will pray for you and who *wills* someone be made well or whole) and there's no doubt in my mind you'll have a seeing baby.'

"Prior to Mary's coming it was easy to resist her suggestion. However, by the time I knew my daughter was blind the promises nearly convinced me. My sister sent books and literature and told me what passages of the Bible to read. She was most insistent that I come to where she lived and go with her to a practitioner. She even told me I could call one on the phone and *believe* and my baby would see.

"Let me tell you, there was a struggle! I called my

38

pastor and talked with him. He told me how wrong I was, but there was a time when I was all set to go to my sister and adopt a new set of beliefs—anything to give sight to my precious children.

"But, I remember standing by the ironing board one morning and suddenly (rather like a light dawning on me) I thought, 'How ridiculous! I have a God I can pray to all by myself. I can get on my knees to him. I don't have to go to a practitioner.' That realization at the ironing board seemed to seal me against further doubt that God was in all of this and that there was a definite purpose in him letting us have these two blind children.

"Naturally, in the beginning we wanted to know why God gave us *two* blind children. But we felt God had definite reasons even though we didn't understand. My husband Hank and I both believed God wanted us to hold on to him, exercise the patience of Job and continue training our children.

"As time went on our answer began to come to us. Hank says it so well: 'It's like God was saying to us, "I want you two closer to me." Boy, that made us both terribly happy because we knew we *would* be closer to God and more devoted to him. This was a big answer for us. He was later to unfold many more reasons and answers to us. Marion and I have been married thirty-five years and we just have to look around us to see the blessings our kids have brought into our lives. They've also brought others into our lives as well—our precious daughter-in-law Janie, our grandson Aaron,

Mary and her husband Steve.

" 'See, all of this was in God's divine plan and it fits now. All our whys have been like parts of a giant puzzle and we can see the whole picture now as it has come together. We're so grateful to God for being so richly blessed.'

"In 1951, Hank and I took both Mary and Ken to the Mayo Clinic. The doctors there confirmed that both the children had the same disease. We were encouraged to 'accept it' and work from this point.

"Though there were heartaches in the years ahead, that acceptance helped us give our kids the freedom to grow. We would see Ken struggling to climb the stairs as a toddler and immediately we would want to go and help him. Many times I've held my hands close to my breast and watched Ken slowly but surely do certain very hard things. It was not easy but we knew he had to learn for himself and he had to always know he was a capable boy.

"I remember one winter when Ken was about eight years old. He wanted to go tobogganing. I can still see him standing at the top of that hill and announcing to us, 'I want to take that sled all the way down by my-self!' We said, 'Huh?' He repeated the sentence in that matter-of-fact way of his and we gave him the sled and he took off like a bird!

"This tobogganing thing was rather tricky. We always had to choose a path where there were only a few trees and then Hank would try and guide him down by telling him where the trees were. It's like Hank says, 'Listen, if Ken wanted to go you didn't say, "Ken, you'll hit a tree, buddy. Better ride behind me." No, we let him go zooming down those snow-covered hills by himself. It hurt. Yes, it hurt very much, but you see, we had to let him do that alone. He howled and laughed all the way down the hill and just had a ball!'

"So, Ken's fun was worth the hurt—until the next time he wanted to go down the hill! But it gave him a sense of accomplishment and of being in control. He needed these successes very much and doing something difficult 'alone' was a big thing for him.

"I can vividly remember the first time Ken ever rode a bike. I was standing in the front yard talking to my sister-in-law. I looked up and there came Ken and my nephew, John, both riding bicycles!

"I thought to myself, 'Oh, my goodness, Ken on a bike!'

"He got off and walked over to me and I asked, 'Ken, how did you ever learn to ride a bike?'

"He answered, 'Well, mother, I just rode it.'

"Many people have asked me how he learned. You see, that's what I don't know. He probably just got on and rode. He had never said, 'I'd like to ride a bike'; or 'I'm learning to ride a bike.' He and his cousin just went down the street and Ken came back riding a bike.

"We probably never felt as sorry for Ken as we did for ourselves. I think that pity was for myself, mainly in those first years when I saw things my friends' children could do that my own son couldn't. I remember I used to go home and cry. Yes, I think mostly the pity was for myself.

"I never saw Ken pitying himself. He believed he could do anything. People were surprised he rode a two-wheeler around the block by himself. In bright sunlight, he could see where the sidewalk stopped and the grass began. He merely saw different shades of gray and kept his bike in the middle of the sidewalk. When other children left toys on the sidewalk he'd always take a tumble because he could not see objects in his way. He'd just pick himself up, move the toys, grumble a bit and get back on his bike. We've asked him many times what he'd do if somebody left a large cart or wagon in his way. He'd answer, 'Well, I'd run into it. So what?'

"When he came to a corner, I believe he could see the different shading of the street ahead and so he'd turn just before he got there. Also, he became very familiar with that one square block.

"But when dusk came Ken could not see any outline at all. He would stumble over things even in the house.

"Now as I look back and read some of the notes the kids wrote in his yearbooks, I take it that Ken gave some of his teachers a rough time in arguments about studies. These 'arguments' held true particularly in his Bible classes. One girl wrote, 'Bible class would have been pretty dull without you making your controversial comments.'

"Ken was a very good student. He has always asked

endless questions. I remember the pastor who worked with him when Ken was eight years old. He remarked to Ken's grandfather, 'Pete Medema, what am I going to do with Ken when he gets into catechism? What am I going to do with the boy?'

"Grandpa answered him with, 'Reverend, don't worry about it. It'll come 'good out' [Dutch expression], I can promise you!'

"Grandpa said a few years later the pastor confessed to him, 'Pete, sometimes that boy asks more questions than I ask of the kids. I've really had to do some studying in that class because Ken was in there.'

"So, he started at eight or nine years old really wanting to know what life was all about. For Ken that meant asking questions.

"With both children being blind, each evening in our home was much the same. I would take one child and go to one room and Hank would take the other in another room. Here we helped them with their homework and read to them. I probably did more of this work with the children than Hank because I could start with them right after school. Also, I was a faster reader than Hank and could speed things up a bit. But Hank and I have split the homework lessons many times.

"It was the same in high school for most of the subjects. By the time Mary got to high school she had quite a few books in Braille and this helped.

"I can remember waiting forever while Ken solved those long geometry problems in his head. I would read the problem and he would respond with, 'O.K.' Then the silence would begin. Sometimes after fifteen minutes he would startle me with, 'Mom, write this down.' I don't know what went on in that head or how he solved those problems, but it blew my mind. It greatly pleased me to see Ken doing well in school and learning things so fast. We knew that Ken loved to read and learn.

"Concerning his musical ability, he had been making up original songs ever since he learned to play the piano. He wrote a song for almost every girl he liked. (He wrote many songs!)

"We had a slight hint that his musical ability was truly promising although we had no idea just how far or in what direction it would ultimately take him.

"Ken's first piano was somewhat of a gift from God. Some friends of ours down the street who were moving came over and asked us if we'd keep their piano for awhile. That was the first we knew that Ken had any ability at the piano. He was about six years old and he just started picking out tunes he had heard. We watched him and saw that he had a memory for tunes and a good sense of rhythm. How he loved the instrument!

"But, six months later, the people came back and we returned their piano. It was a blow for us because we saw what that piano had done for him. And we realized then that he *needed* a piano. Hank's father and brother got together and bought him one. None of us then had any idea where that piano would lead Ken. Even with all his fantasies and wild imagination, I would go so far as to say that Ken himself never dreamed music would carry him on exciting adventures through life, and because of his special God-given talents, he would be able to carry thousands of people with him.

"Ken enjoyed not only his piano for he had his own record player, tape recorder and he built his own tuner when he was in junior high. With all this equipment in the living room we had a mass of wires and cords everywhere. He put all this together by himself.

"One day he asked Hank, 'Hey, dad, can we have some speakers upstairs? Let's run the wires through the partitions and up the walls.' So, Ken and his dad drilled holes in the ceiling, ran the necessary wires up through the holes, and we had music all over the house. Ken loved nothing more than being surrounded by music.

"Because of Ken's unique ministry I am asked many various questions, but I would have to say that the most frequently asked question is, 'How does a blind person learn music?'

"Well, I can speak only for my own son. The usual methods of learning and coping with problems in music had not always been available to Ken, but he learned to play the piano by listening to tape recordings or reading music written in Braille. He would feel with his left hand and learn to play the right-hand part, and then feel with the right hand and learn to play the left.

"Ken knew that at the time he was learning music, Braille literature was limited and a very slow process—for Ken it was too slow so he supplemented Braille with an oral method. His music teacher would record the music on tape at a very slow tempo, pointing out verbally the dynamics and all the markings which are printed on the score. After listening to these tapes over and over, Ken would play the piece of music at the proper tempo. He learned much new music by listening to tapes. Through all of his college study he continued to use Braille music when it was practical.

"Because Ken is on the road so much I don't have the opportunity to see him very often. His father and I are, of course, staunch fans and play some of his recordings almost every day.

"I am so very proud of Ken and when I have the chance to go to one of his concerts it's a real treat. Each new concert is so exciting for me because I get to hear him so seldom. But when Ken is up on a stage playing the piano and singing, he's not 'my son.' I never think, 'Oh, look, my son is up there performing.' Rather he becomes someone who is just spiritually thrilling my soul completely!"

4

Lord, Are You Looking for Me?

Lord, are you looking for me?
And what makes you think you can find me?
I can hide rather well if I want to.
I can hide rather well if I try.
Lord, are you looking for me?
And what makes you think you can . . .

We were walking to church and I remember my steps were getting almost as big as my dad's for I was now a junior in high school. As we walked I heard people coming down the sidewalk going to church and I heard the bells ringing. One of the local churches even had organ music and the sound rose from the steeple. An image came to mind that had come many times in the last few years. I knew enough Scripture to be dangerous and I thought to myself, "These people are like sheep. They're being led to slaughter."

My favorite description for the church at that time was "the edifice of ignorance." For you see, *I* was enlightened! I knew in man's search for purpose and meaning he had called his ideal many things: Allah,

Jehovah, and a lot of other names. I thought that one God was as good as another, one search for truth as good as another—but *they* didn't. I couldn't understand that others could be so limited and narrow.

When I was a child I used to listen to the bells as they rang on Sunday mornings, and everytime they'd ring I felt good because Sunday was a fun day.

When they rang during my senior high school years I sank deeper into the covers on my bed and didn't want to get up. The bells heralded that coming hour when I would have to sing those songs and listen to that man preach again. I even made token responses—I actually prayed and sang solos in the church. I talked a very pious language, but I knew beyond the shadow of a doubt that I was no Christian. I didn't address God because I didn't believe he existed.

Occasionally at a Youth for Christ gathering I was disturbed by meeting a very committed Christian teen-ager. But then the feeling would leave. I'm not bothered by things very long.

Anyway, I wanted to play the part of the heretic. So, Ken Medema was in "heresy corner." In addition to associating with my musical friends, I tended to hang around the kids at school who were smart-alecky and discontented with what their churches were teaching. I was very conscious of running at this stage—of running away from what people were saying to me.

I ran by denying the intelligence and the validity of a Christian's experience. I ran by diving into the aesthetics of church life—that is: What kind of music are we making? Let's be sure we have excellent music. I shall be eternally grateful I never had the chance to pursue that any further than I did for had I become church organist I think it would have ruined the spirit in my church.

I was concerned about good music and this concern was, I believe, a way of running from God. I didn't want to hear God. I wanted to hear music! And this is where all the conflicts came between my parents and me. You see, I wanted to have the freedom at home to say whatever I wanted. I wanted the freedom not to go to church. In short, I wanted no demands on me concerning religious life. But those demands were made anyway. I had to go to church and was even pressured to sing in the choir.

Then I went to a Christian high school so I had to take Bible courses, church history courses, and sing in chapel. In general, I had to play the part of a "nice religious kid." I was never so happy as the day I left high school and could go to Michigan State University where I could be the liberal, enlightened humanist who knew everything! I started out that way—but my dreams didn't take me as far as I wanted them to, for as I will explain later, I met a girl who showed me a different way.

I didn't hide in many of the places my song says:

I can hide on top of the world in an airplane,
Leave the bums and the slums
To rot down below.
I can hide in the sanctity of a Sunday morning.

Well, I *did* hide in aloneness in my woods and by my lake, but I fought hard to keep God out of my life.

I wasn't too happy with my parents, either. There were many things I resented about them. One was our not being able to talk. I don't blame them for it because they really didn't know how. They could do it now, but at the time they were afraid, and because they were afraid they backed away.

I think the biggest reason we couldn't talk was that in my parents' home when they were growing up, you didn't talk about things. You obeyed your parents! You followed the rules, you toed the mark and if you didn't you were clobbered! So, they had not grown up in the freedom to discuss things like, "How am I going to react to this or that?" or "Do I like this or not?" You don't discuss it—you just do it!

So, when I came along as a high school student and started asking questions like, "Why is it so important for me to go to church?" or "Why can't I have the freedom to choose the friends I want and go where I want and come in when I want?" or "Why do you resent my religious understanding being different from yours?" they were not able to discuss these questions with me. I wouldn't have minded it so much if they had talked honestly with me even though their answers would probably have struck me as narrow-minded, conservative, and fundamentalistic.

But you see, they could not admit incompetence in an area, so I resented them. I realize now that a great deal of the resenting was unnecessary and very childish on my part. Now that Mary and I are both out of the house, on our own, and given to the Lord, we have become much freer to talk. I think part of the reason for the change and the freedom is their security in having done "all right" by us.

But, before we reached this great place where we are now, we went through some difficult times. My first two years in college were characterized by deception. I led my parents to believe I was going to church regularly and that I had met some families in the church there at college. They thought all was well with my spiritual life.

I lied just as easily as taking a step. I found that once you start lying, each succeeding lie becomes easier. My conscience would sleep beautifully through all the lies I wanted to tell.

Now, as a Christian of some thirteen years, I cannot have the revulsion that some people feel about lying. There are those who could not lie. It would just tear them up inside to lie. I know that were it not for a head-level conviction that lying is hurtful and dangerous, I would still be doing it. Part of it is, of course, the inevitable human fear of getting caught and part of it, too, is the idea that I know in my mind but not down on a gut level that a Christian shouldn't lie. However, I wish I had that added protection of the gut-level fear of doing something wrong. I'm not afraid of it any more.

In contrast, my wife, Jane, is more naturally frank and open. Many things still tempt me because at one time I found them so easy to do that they became a part of my behavior pattern. So, I have to constantly fight temptations harder than Jane.

I talk to a lot of teenagers who say, "Well, I'll get it straightened out next month or next year." They're always going to get it straightened out, always going to get things settled. The problem is that the longer you tolerate undesirable behavior, the more comfortable it gets and the harder it is then to erase it.

Anyway, deception was very much a part of my life. What is so beautiful is that after I became a Christian, my parents and I had a confession time—I told them about the lying and they knew and somehow way back then I *knew* they knew but I had to keep up the front. They were aware I was lying but they wouldn't tell me, "Son, you're lying to us."

My problem with the church centered around the fact that I was really not interested much in what our church had to say. My spirit simply never said yes to the things I was learning in church.

There were just two reasons for my being in church at all. The first was, I had to be there. Beyond that the church provided a place for enjoyable, aesthetic experiences. After all, there were organ recitals and sometimes the choir did some fairly good music.

I realize now that my pastor and teachers really loved me and they demonstrated love to me. However, I was unwilling to accept it. At the time I was in junior and senior high school, the Christian Reformed Church, I believe, was very conservative and very unbending. It did not have, to me, the nature of an open, loving community, but today it is much more open and much more receptive, and aggressively looking for people to love. I think this is partially because of having caught the sense of "opening up" that characterizes much of the Christian community today.

I started asking lots of questions in classes at school and I started identifying myself with the three or four kids who always sat in heresy corner. I rejected, not only Calvinist theology, but also the Bible as the Word of God. I rejected even the notion that God existed. Rather, I believed that somewhere there was truth and meaning and purpose and any way you could find it was O.K.

I went back to my high school many years later and told my Bible teacher that when I was in his class I was not a Christian. Although I could not see the expression on his face, I believe he was surprised and perhaps dismayed.

At the time, neither the school nor the church was able to speak to me about game-playing. Also, I honestly think that had the school or the church been willing to listen to my questions, encouraged me to go out on a limb, I would have felt the freedom there that I experienced in Heather's studio. If only I had been allowed to ask questions, to doubt, to deny—"How can this be! This is ridiculous!" But at that time the freedom wasn't there and maybe providence would have had it so.

I think the healthiest thing to come out of this experience was the asking of questions. I realized something which many of my friends did not, at least at the time. I realized it is necessary for some people to repeatedly ask those basic questions about life. Questions like: Where am I going? Who am I? Who is God? What is God like, if he exists? What's it all about? I knew I needed to ask those questions and no one could stop me. It was this realization that perhaps served as a springboard for really coming to the point of letting myself be found by a loving God.

The whole conflict was, I feel now, a very healthy, positive, providential happening because of the way it ended. I feel that I have been enabled to empathize with people who ask questions, who doubt, and who disbelieve because I have gone through such questioning myself. That's not the only way, but it was the way God led me.

And so this song ends with the lines that I believe I felt many years ago:

> Lay off, Jesus,
> Why do you want me so!
> Lord, are you looking for me?
> And what makes you think you can find me?

However, it wasn't long until I came to a fork in the road.

5

~~~~~~~~~~~~~~~~~~~~~ *Fork in the Road*

Stop right here, there's a fork in the road.
I don't think you want to get lost.
One way leads to a potter's field,
The other way leads to a Cross.

Didn't Robert Frost write a poem about a fork in a road? Didn't he say, "Two roads diverged in a wood, and I, I took the one less traveled by, and that has made all the difference"? Well, I came to that Y in the road in my own life.

During my first years in college I went to some meetings of various religious organizations—Methodist Youth Fellowship, InterVarsity, Campus Crusade. They all turned me off! The kids were nice, but they were too placid and sweet and peaceful and kind and good and pious and religious and Christian, and I really didn't like that. Besides, there were no ashtrays!

About this time in my life, I met a girl named Jane Smith who was a tremendous musician. She was the most accomplished accompanist we had in the student body, and her ability at the piano commanded my respect. Also, we had some friends in common. There was a whole group of us who would go to coffee together at the student union, and we'd spend many hours pounding the table and talking about one thing and another. We always got around to religion somehow, and I would engage in this long polemic against belief in the supernatural.

Now, although Jane is a tremendous talker and can spin out an argument with as much ease as an expert seamstress weaves thread into an article of clothing, she never put me down for my questions. She never told me my thinking wasn't straight. In all the discussions and the arguments she always had a positive, loving, caring attitude toward me. Also, she seemed to know that I was hurting.

This freedom to ask questions was something I had never had with Christians before. I had experienced it with Heather and I had experienced it among my musical friends, but this was something new. The freedom to question without reproach was a real turn-on and I liked talking to Jane because I could be myself.

Jane and I were in a class together, Recreational Music, and the class was designed to help music students learn techniques of teaching folk-dancing, folk-singing, and musical games. The teacher knew I would not be able to do those things because I couldn't see the motions so she asked Jane to help me. I say now, from this vantage point, "Lord, I'll bet she didn't even know that you were using her."

After I became a Christian, I began to wonder about marrying Jane and I began to think it just might happen. I remember one time when I had gone home at the end of summer school. Before leaving for Grand Rapids, I had said to Jane, "You know, it's really good we have this relationship that's so platonic. Neither one of us is tied down, so we can be together and yet date other people. We can be good friends and not have any romantic entanglements to bind us."

I think that bothered her because she knew partially it wasn't true. She knew I had a crush on her and my statement probably bothered her ego a bit. But shortly after I got home Jane wrote me a letter—a rather "torchy" letter. The moment I received it, I boarded a bus for Lansing. Upon reaching her house I asked her to walk to the park with me. We sat on a bench and put our feet up and talked about what it would be like to get married. From that day on I *knew* it would happen.

And two years later in June 1965, a month after my college graduation, it indeed did happen. We got married at two o'clock in the afternoon so that I could see Jane's outline coming down the aisle of the church. But I couldn't see Jane's features. I just knew she had dark hair and I could see her outline as she stood beside me at the church. It was beautiful!

From the time of our marriage, we've made our pilgrimage together, so anything I say in succeeding chapters about "we" will mean Jane and me. Jane and I have gone to the same places together. We've absorbed and doubted and received and believed the same things together so much that it is hard for me to talk about *my* journey without hers. I'm sure she would say the same.

I don't recall any major problems regarding our being married. However, her grandparents didn't like the idea of her marrying a blind person. They said, "How will he ever work?" In fact, her grandmother said, "How will he take you to the hospital when you get pregnant?" It was a legitimate question, and at the time her biggest concern. By the way, we went to the hospital in a taxi when our son Aaron was born!

Anyway, back to college days. I went with Jane to her home several times so we could work on the musical material. I met Jane's dad, Dr. Truett Smith, her mother, Mary Lee, her brother, Buddy, and her sister, Ginger. Jane's dad was the director of the Baptist Student Union at Michigan State University and also the pastor of the First Baptist Church of East Lansing, a small church primarily made up of students.

As I became closer to her family I felt the same kind of freedom that I felt with Jane. Having come from a very ordered, very organized and very efficient Dutch family, my impression of the Smith household was that it was total chaos all the time! Everybody was always talking. Meals never seemed planned—they just sort of happened. We never worried much about time schedules. We just sat around and did what we wanted to do until the very last minute, then we'd rush off to go somewhere. But that atmosphere was delightful because I appreciated coming into the less organized, less efficient, less scheduled, less regimented kind of family structure.

Jane's father was a man whom I respected immensely. For some reason, I had always associated Baptist ministers with a lack of intellectual prowess. But here was a man who was as mentally alert, as intellectually competent as any teacher I had had at the university. His mind worked in channels which I had never even dreamed of before, and he talked about the Christian gospel in ways that were new to me. As we talked not so much about doctrine but rather about relationship, it really *was* good news for me.

I argued. I had to keep on fighting but I inhaled it all nevertheless. Having been around the family for some time and having experienced the freedom with Jane, I began to feel within myself a change of attitude toward the idea of being a Christian. I began to think, "There *are* Christians who are neat. They're not so bad. Maybe I can be one." But, I wasn't ready yet to take the step.

Jane was not attending her parents' church for she was the interim music and youth director at another Baptist church. I went with her to church on Sundays simply because I wanted to be with her. They didn't know I wasn't a Christian so they asked me to sing and pray and do just about everything but preach! It dawned on me, gradually, that I was doing the same thing now that I had done before—I was deceiving people. I was leading them to believe I was a Christian, but I had never made a commitment.

Really, there was no aesthetic reason for me to like

this church. The music was country. Most of the people were from nearby states and were blue-collar workers who had come to Michigan because they couldn't get jobs elsewhere. For me, a music student who had been used to the classics, the music was awful. I thought the only class that existed in that church was the class *I* added! *They* needed what I had to give! But, you know something? The people loved me and were so warm and kind, gentle and affirming, that I was drawn to them.

Well, all these things began to come together and one night I realized that a change had to be made. I *knew* that somehow my relationships and attitudes could be made right, and I knew reconciliation would take place with my parents. So one night in my dormitory room, I got on my knees and I simply said, "Lord, I'm gonna quit fighting. I've never really prayed to you and believed before, but I'm doing it now."

There was no thunder, no lightning, no tears, no tongues—just a guy praying. It wasn't like, "Oh, Lord, I'm such a miserable, wretched, awful sinner. How could you ever have loved someone so terrible as I?" Nor was it, "Lord, I'm at the very end of my rope and I'm going to commit suicide. Please deliver me." It was simply, "Lord, I want to quit fighting and I'm going to believe that it's so."

After my prayer in the dorm, I called Jane and told her I had prayed. We went to her parents' home and talked to them for a long time. There was great excitement. A short time later I walked the aisle of Jane's church and made a profession of faith. I told the pastor

I had not been a Christian and I wanted the church to know. I wanted to be baptized. It was a most beautiful experience. I'll never forget the thrill of baptism by immersion in water, realizing I was picturing my death to an old life and the beginning of new life.

I remember thinking, "I know now that I am clean. I know that I am new. I know that I am forgiven. I know that as many times as I may fail, I have new status. And I know this baptism in itself did not give me new status, but it is my way of telling everyone that I realize and I appropriate the fact that I have this new, clean, made-whole life." That was the point at which the new journey started.

Now, back to the words of the song. Somewhere in the middle there are lines that say:

> Jesus, it's a very hard road that You walk,
> Some people try to follow You but it's
>   little more than talk.
> The road leads through the wilderness of
>   human need and pain.
> You put Your hands on the broken hearts
>   of men,
> Looked into their dying faces and
>   gave them hope again.

I determined that I did not want a limited kind of Christian experience. I wanted the sky! I wanted God's best for me! So, I started by trying to mend some old things, and the first thing I had to mend was my relationship with my parents. I debated and worked through it for a couple of months.

So many questions came to mind: How do I tell them? Will they be offended that I have become a Baptist? Will they be offended that by conviction and by belief in Baptist doctrine I have embraced what they said about the freedom of the individual to interpret the Word?

I believed all this was right and it rang bells for me but I was concerned about their response. I wondered further: Will they be annoyed with me? Will they bring up to me all the lying I have done before? I didn't know and I was afraid.

After a time I did talk with them, and it was warm and loving and wonderful. I realized then that one of the things that happens when a person settles things with God is that he becomes enabled to settle things with other people. The reconciliation that took place between me and my mom and dad—the making whole, the making right—was for me a mini-drama. It was as if the whole story of redemption had been narrowed down, put in a thimble, and brought to that living room. Then, it was as though it had been released and exploded all over that house. The whole house was so full of redemption that the walls couldn't contain it. I felt so good—like a balloon ready to pop!

I started off my Christian life with glorious ideals—I was going to study the Bible every day, and I was going to pray and witness. That lasted for awhile. Then things started settling down to reality and I had to cope with the fact that I am lazy, that I want to get away with as little work as possible. I had to cope with the fact that I really don't like to do anything consistently. And I had to cope with the fact that I was still my egocentric self who wanted to be on top of everything and come off always looking like the very best.

However, one thing was always firm in my mind. No matter how lazy I was in my devotional life, no matter how seldom the prayers, or how poor my attitude about servanthood, one thing was always firm. And now as I come to the end of my song I remember what was *always* there:

> Beneath the cross of Jesus I'm gonna take
> my stand.
> The shadow of a mighty rock within a weary
> land.
> A home within the wilderness, a rest upon
> the way,
> From the burning of the noontide heat and
> the burden of the day.
> —Elizabeth C. Clephane, alt.

Stop right here. There's a fork in the road.

6

~~~~~~~~~~~~~~~~~~~~~~~~~~~~~ *Touching*

I shivered as I walked down the hospital corridor. I usually experienced this same reaction whenever I confronted a new patient whom I'd never seen before. This was a particularly scary one.

He was not your ordinary run-of-the mill psychiatric hospital patient. This young man was in training to be a psychologist and had worked for two years at another hospital. The pressures of his work and his long-term instability had capsized his boat and he was now in the admissions ward at the Essex County Hospital in New Jersey.

He was hallucinating, his talk made no sense at all, he was inclined toward violence, the ward staff detested him and some ding-a-ling doctor had gotten the idea that music therapy would be the cure-all.

My patient was not allowed off the ward because he was a security risk; therefore, I found myself in a noisy, crowded admissions ward sitting in an unused dining room with a portable record player and a "crazy" man. What do I do now?

I tried to talk but talking was useless. My friend was not at all in contact with reality. He got up several times during that first thirty-minute session and paced around the room, slapping the walls, yelling at me, protesting against his imprisonment, talking to people who weren't there—in general, scaring the life out of me!

Somewhere toward the end of the session (I can't even remember what was playing on the record player) he sat down next to me at the table and listened for what seemed a very long time. Actually, I think it was eight measures worth. He turned to me and I could feel the heat of his face against my own.

"That's a nice song. I've always liked that one. Let's play that one again. Will you come tomorrow?"

"Yes," I said, "I'll come tomorrow and tomorrow and tomorrow and all the weeks that lie ahead of us. I'll come. I'll play music. I'll sing songs. I'll help you build bridges. This time is your time is my time is our time."

When Jane and I got married we left Michigan to go to Indiana where I assumed the position of director of music therapy at Fort Wayne State Hospital and Training Center. My job was to begin a program of music therapy at this institution. It was a challenge and Jane and I were excited about our new work.

Jane, after working for awhile in music therapy, took the post of in-service training director for the activities therapy department. Her job was to provide training for nonprofessionals who worked directly with patients.

I owe a great deal to music therapy. Much of what I

have learned about hurting and touching and the specifics of reaching out to people, and much of what I have learned about how to open my own life to the risks of relationship, I learned as a music therapist.

Music therapy is the prescribed use of music and music experiences in the rehabilitation of physically or mentally disabled persons.

Now, let's amplify that just a little bit. The basic premise that underlies all of music therapy practice is that music does things *for* people and *to* them. The things that music does are healing, connecting, restoring—all directed toward reality.

Let me give you a few examples. That first position as director of music therapy for mentally retarded at a hospital for multiple handicapped children and adults revealed to me a range of retardation from mild to severe. All the patients were braindamaged and some were orthopedically handicapped. All sorts of physical disabilities were represented among the patient population.

We found that music experience was able: First, to assist our patients in developing better physical coordination as in folk dance, square dance, circle games, instrument playing and more. Second, we found that the retarded person, who is inclined to feel a lack of positive self-image, felt a success experience in music ("Look, mom, I can play the trumpet!" or the autoharp, or the piano). We discovered this contributed immensely to his feeling of being a person of worth.

Third, we found that making music together brought about an increased awareness of others, their needs and problems, and particularly their identity. For example, "Who is the person next to you? What is his name? Can you hear his instrument? Can you hear his voice?"

Fourth, we discovered that music provided the way for our patients to engage in here-and-now oriented behavior without being put on a spot. I'm talking about the children and adults who tried to escape the discomforts of reality by stepping into worlds of fantasy. These people were beating drums, singing songs, listening to tunes, remembering tunes, standing up, sitting down, taking a dance step, forming a circle—every exterior influence motivated musically to help heal and rebuild human beings.

We discovered, also, that verbal material which had to be learned, such as how to tie shoes, what traffic lights meant, and other important, necessary tasks, could be grasped more effectively when put into songs. These songs provided not only a way to remember, but a positive contact for learning.

These principles provided some of the framework for my music therapy practice in Indiana. Music therapy has been an organized discipline since 1950. There are many colleges throughout the nation which offer music therapy in their curriculum. A student receives a music degree with heavy emphasis on courses in psychology, special education, physiology, social work and other behavioral science courses.

After leaving Indiana in 1967, we returned to MSU for graduate study. Between Jane and me we juggled three graduate assistantships, several part-time jobs, two class schedules, homework and the responsibilities of caring for a new baby boy. Jane's master's degree is in music education and my graduate study is in both music therapy and applied voice.

Perhaps the most exciting of my positions in the music therapy field was that which I assumed in June of 1969. I served as assistant director of music and creative arts therapy at Essex County Hospital Center in Cedar Grove, New Jersey. Later on I became the director of the program.

In New Jersey I worked in a psychiatric hospital with persons whose disability ranged from mild neurosis to severe psychotic disturbance. There were persons who merely had some uncomfortable, unpleasant hangups. Then, there were those who had spent years of their lives totally locked away in a fantasy world unable to cope with reality in any form. Music very often allows us to break through the layers of fantasy and illusion with a reality-oriented stimulus.

I remember the patient who sat on the piano bench and imitated the notes I was playing. He had not spoken to anyone nor had he responded to any stimulus in years and yet he heard and was able to repeat those notes. I knew for certain that he was making contact with reality on some level.

In the psychiatric hospital, we relied heavily on the premise that music brings people together. Music provides a way for you and me to come together and to do something together that is positive. It involves both of us working together with precise timing, having to listen to each other and be aware of mistakes. All of this heightens our sensitivity to the presence of the other person.

I worked with psychologists and psychiatrists as a co-therapist, a member of the treatment team. I learned a great deal about approaches to psychotherapy and from this experience I drew not only material that was valuable for my own life, but also concepts that were to direct my thinking about the use of music in therapy, in worship, in communication and in teaching.

In therapy groups I conducted, I learned a great deal about touching. I particularly remember a big, tall, muscular street-kid from Newark who was almost non-verbal when he came to the hospital. His relationship to school was a negative one—breaking windows and hitting teachers. I announced to the group that we were going to put on a rock show and I wanted original material. "Anybody want to write songs?" I asked. There was no response. After three weeks, however, this boy handed me a wrinkled-up piece of paper that had obviously been in the wastebasket once. My secretary read the words:

> Touching is a very hard thing to do,
> Seems like you can't get to me
> And I can't get to you.
> What are we afraid of?
> Why can't we share?
> We're never gonna make it
> If we can't learn to care.

> It takes so long to bust our little shell
> When you're all alone
> The world's a living hell.

These lyrics became a kind of theme song for the musical that year. I composed the tunes and the kids wrote the words.

Two years later, after we had struggled together, sung together, lit the stage together, worked the sound system together, talked together and learned to love each other, this youngster, nearing his discharge date, wrote me some more words:

> Maybe if I try I can say I love you.
> Maybe if I try I can say I care.
> Maybe if we work it out together we can learn
>   to see each other.
> Maybe if we talk about it we can learn to share.

I don't know where he is now nor what he is doing, but I do know that in two years of therapy he came a long way and much of it had to do with his experience with music and with other people in the context of a warm singing, group experience.

It would take too much space to list all case histories and maybe I'll write a book someday about my experiences with specific people, but let me mention just one other.

I told you about the boy who wrote the songs, but then there was the ten-year-old autistic child who was so withdrawn and introverted that his speech, rather than being communicative, consisted of only echoes of what other people had to say. If I said, "Hello," he would say, "Hello." If I said, "Go away," then he would say, "Go away." He could neither answer yes or no nor tell me what an object was. But, after six months of working with him in music, playing the piano, singing to him, walking him around the room pointing out objects to him, always taking him back to the piano to play, playing duets, making up music to his pounding—in all this we were able to carry on some sort of reasonable conversation.

When I returned to the hospital for a visit a few years later, I was pleased to note that this little fellow had not regressed, but rather had improved.

The work is not always so rewarding. Sometimes progress is painfully slow. Sometimes patients will remain in hospitals for years and all we can do is maintain a level of behavior that prevents them from completely disintegrating. But no matter how slow the progress, no matter how unrewarding the work, we have an obligation to every person who is disabled. It is our obligation to help him become as fine a human being as he is able to become.

Some of you will be interested in learning more about the field of music therapy. The National Association for Music Therapists is located in the city of Lawrence, Kansas. I'm certain that if you care to write to the Association, the office staff will be glad to provide you with

71

brochures and other informative material that can help clarify what you want to know about this most exciting use of music.

My experiences as a music therapist gave me a definite perspective on the place of music in person-to-person communication. So then it was natural that I left my music therapy directorship in 1973 to venture out into a full-time singing ministry so that I could apply the principles I had learned as a therapist to my work in churches.

Therefore, I developed the notion of a goal-oriented time together: What do we want to do together? How can music help us do it?

Some of my primary goals are: First, to come to know more about who God is; second, to come to know more about who I am; third, to come to know you better; fourth, to be able to touch you more easily; fifth, to be able to come away with a **good** feeling about myself and you; sixth, to be able to grasp a sense of my place in God's plan for world reconciliation.

In working toward meeting these goals sometimes we sing together, sometimes I sing to you. Often you give me ideas for a song and I write it on the spot. At other times I ask you to make up words or new words to old tunes. We clap, stomp, jump, skip, gallop and dance together. Sometimes we listen to someone else's music, sometimes I make music while you all rub shoulders, shake hands. Other times we just sit quietly holding hands and listen to songs about crying.

But whatever the medium, whatever I'm doing, all

this needs to be directed toward a goal. The goal is like the punch line of a joke, and the thing we do, the method, is what needs the punch line.

In a sense I am still a music therapist because I am constantly working out, in and for myself, for you, for the others who join me in a concert or a worship service, some of the problems that were mentioned above. I am still working toward those goals everywhere I go.

The exciting and dramatically different thing about my work now is that I have the freedom to deal with all of these things in the context of our relationship to a loving God. Therapy, then, can become a working out of our walk with Christ and this, I feel, is the most exciting place in which I could ever find myself. I like what I do. I am happy in my work and I will always be indebted to my training for giving me that unique perspective that I believe only the therapist can have.

Ken mastered
most of the usual
childhood activities . . .

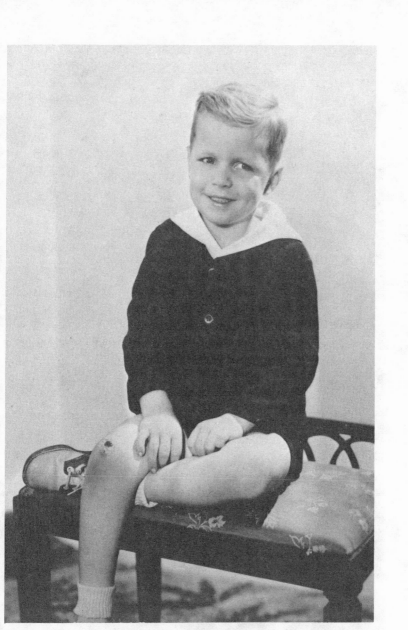

. . . but not without a few bumps and bruises.

Ken's Mom and Dad outside their home in Grand Rapids, Michigan.

Ken enjoys relating
to his audience at a children's
concert in New Jersey.

Piano practice is interrupted by the family pet, Satin Psyche.

Coming home is always a special treat after several weeks on tour.

Sharing a good book with
Jane and making a
pot of coffee are two favorite
experiences in Ken's
At-Home world.

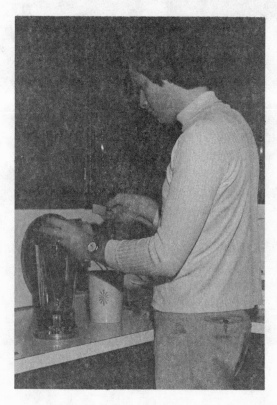

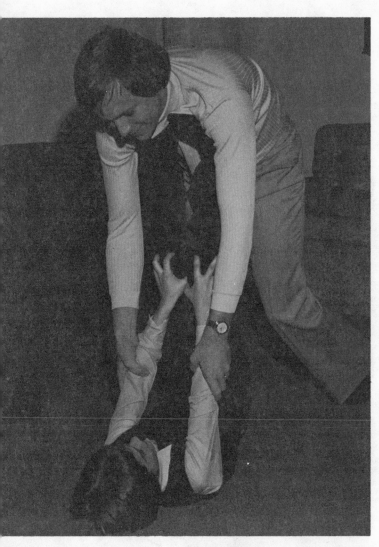

Ken and his nine-year-old son Aaron
enjoy a typical romp on the living room floor.

Ken, Jane and Aaron Medema

7

•••••••••••••••••••••••••••••••••••••• *Intermission*

We have just finished *Touching*, and as the notes die away I know it is time for an intermission. We've been sitting here at this piano too long and we need to stretch our legs. So while we take an intermission I would like to share with you some perspectives I have gained in working with the church. I would like to talk to you about my feelings concerning music in the church, the use of improvising, the dangers of emotional manipulation, the importance of the will, the place of honesty, and the Christian artist.

Why don't you come outside with me and we'll stand by the backstage door. There's a breeze out there and with the sweat I've worked up I need a breeze. I can always talk better with a cup of coffee in my hand. So have a cup with me and we'll relax a moment, sip our coffee and talk.

A lot of people have asked me what I think about music in the church. I suppose they think because I'm a performer I'm an expert. That's not really true. A real expert on church music has a vast background in musicology, has been in lots of churches, and has hurt and sweated and groaned with people when they needed music to help them confront their disillusionment. Such an expert has a big heart. I don't think I qualify, but still they ask me.

What do I tell them? First, a musical style is an essentially neutral thing. I have read numerous articles and books that have appeared in recent years stating that the rock beat is the "devil's beat," and the pulsating rhythms of current popular music must inevitably lead one into sinful behavior. I simply do not buy this way of thinking. There are some styles that bother us and some styles that don't.

If you want to make noise about the rock style and its rhythmic beat and its association with sin, listen to a song such as John Peterson's, "It Took a Miracle." The chords in that song are very similar to the chords in numerous popular songs of the '40s and '50s. It really is not a long jump from "Somebody Loves Me" to "It Took a Miracle."

That is one example of hundreds I could give. My point is that when we talk about a musical style we are talking about something that becomes charged with meaning and significance only as we allow it to be so charged. Apart from that charge it is neutral.

Which Reformation theologian was it who complained that the devil has all the good tunes? With the conviction that a style is neutral, I maintain if a style serves as a suitable package for a message, then you should use it! The worth of a musical style depends on three considerations: Who is the music intended to glorify? What are the motivations of the individuals using the style? Will the listeners be able to understand this medium as a package for the message under consideration?

God created the human body to respond to rhythm. Because we associate loud music and rock-type rhythms with sensuous, sexual behavior, this does not mean that it has always been or must always be so. God did not distort those things. We did. The Lord can use rock, jazz, folk, blues, ballad, symphony, the minuet or a Sousa march—but, these same styles can also be used for the glorification of the flesh to promote immorality.

I am concerned about an aesthetic experience. I don't mean simply that we put the words to a song in the easiest style, for the style is also part of the message. Without style what we have is a very true, but perhaps less interesting story.

If we choose a musical style that accentuates the truth of the message, then I believe the response in most cases will be positive. I have rarely received negative responses from concerts I have done, whether from the eighty-year-old grandmother at the youth concert or the sixteen-year-old "in" kids at a senior citizens' show. Somehow people seem to feel that what I do works. It has integrity. I don't fully understand it but I use a variety of styles and I am very conscious of trying to match the idiom to the message. The style must be compatible with the message.

Now another question I'm often asked, "What about instruments? When you perform you use a piano. You don't have guitars, drums or amplifiers." That's true, I don't. I feel a need to return to simplicity of texture, not that my piano texture is necessarily simple. But, I feel a need to return to textures that don't depend on twenty-seven instruments, half as many amplifiers, wah-wahs, fuzz boxes and quadraphonic sound systems. Don't get me wrong, I respect those things. I admire them whenever they're used *tastefully*.

"Ooops," you say, "what's 'tastefully'?" I can't tell you what is tasteful for you. I can tell you what it is for me. Because of my classical background, I was programed to have some kind of sense of proportion. That is, things ought to fit. Nothing should be out of context. Don't let the drum just bang; don't let the guitar just whine away all night. Keep it all in perspective. One thing balancing another. This is my criterion for taste.

If music is in what I consider good taste, then I don't mind any number of instruments, amplifiers and electronic gadgets. However, I still feel the need to return to simple textures. A piano and a voice. A guitar and a voice. A guitar and a flute. One stop on an organ. A recorder. An autoharp and a folk singer. A mandolin.

These kinds of basic people-to-people textures and idioms can communicate so much of intimacy and honesty. Sometimes I wish we could get out from behind the drums and the pipe organs and the stained-glass windows and the guitars and the clothes—and just stand facing each other and sing the basic human cry, "I love you."

And then there's the improvising that is a joy, a gift from God—a necessity in all I do with music. How it has developed I cannot fully articulate, but I shall try and explain its place in my music as best I can.

I've always been able to improvise instrumentally. To play by ear. To pick up a tune and play it on the piano. To do as the jazz players do. We call it in the business "take a ride." That is, to build upon a melody a superstructure which consists of ornaments, trills, turns, runs, scales—you need only to listen to a good jazz trio to hear what I mean.

I have occasionally puttered with making up little ditties, little bits of song, little rambling bits of unconnected, nonrhyming poetry. Nothing much ever came of it until 1971. At a meeting in Madison, New Jersey, where I had no song to fit the preacher's message, I improvised "Fork in the Road" almost exactly as one hears it recorded on my first album.

There was some improvising that went on between then and 1972. But in May of that year I attended an evangelistic conference in Philadelphia and heard my friend Jack Taylor speak on the subject of Moses throwing down the rod. I had a real surrendering kind of experience and it was then I noticed my improvising had increased tremendously. I found myself wanting to do it and feeling responsible for doing it. I began looking forward to building songs on a pastor's message or a speaker's speech.

"Can it be taught?" some people ask. Well, maybe. Maybe you have to have a combination of the gift and the training. Improvising has provided for me a most stimulating environment in which to work. I never have to depend on canned material.

Quite often it is my function in a conference to spend the week summarizing, reinforcing, and repeating what speakers say—bringing their words together, pulling out their meanings and bringing those meanings together in juxtaposition. This is one of my favorite challenges in all of life. I think I am a better responder than initiator. I am always more comfortable responding to what somebody tells me. Sometimes when there is a desire on my part to respond but not much to respond to, it is extremely frustrating.

So negative and positive situations are useful inputs for what I improvise. Perhaps this is nothing new. But maybe the combination of a musical language with poetry, improvised on the spot, is a new approach.

One of the sources for my music is my own inner self—"Who am I? What's going on in me? How do I respond to myself and my environment? What makes me angry? What makes me ache? Why don't I ache enough? What makes me think I really know how to love?" Questions like these that ramble around in my mind and heart come out in my music.

People have remarked to me, "Medema, you are incredibly honest." And I suppose my feeling is that if I want someone to be honest with me, then I must be honest first. Yes, I am honest in my music. I am honest because it does me good to confess and it does you good to hear. It does you good to see me take the risk. And so, in one of my songs, I say of the church:

If this is not a place where tears are understood,
Where can I go to cry?
If this is not a place where my spirit can take wings,
Where can I go to fly?

The church needs to be a place where I can cry to you and you to me. You will not despise me for my crying and I will not despise you for your sinning and you will not reject me for my foolishness. I will not refuse you entrance to my heart because you disappoint me. I will demand of you the highest you are capable of, but I will not let you down when you "don't get there." You will expect of me the best I can be, but you'll not turn me out when I just can't make it. Rather you'll love me over and over again.

So, in this climate of honesty, affirming love, we can speak to each other and remove some of our masks. I have discovered that in these conditions the Word of God becomes uniquely and fantastically *alive*.

I recall a phrase an instructor used at Union Seminary where my wife is a student: "We so often spend time exegeting the Bible that we do not let the Bible exegete us." But you see, the Bible can interpret us only when we are in an environment where we are vulnerable and open. To the degree that we are those things, we become free.

Am I a "professional" Christian artist? There is a sense in which I *am* a professional just as anyone who is trained and adequate for his work is a professional.

To the extent that "professionalism" takes away the amateurish thrill that I find in my work or in life, I must reject that professionalism. If *professional* means skilled, trained, able—then, I gladly accept the identity "professional musician."

Mr. Robert Shaw made this remark and I shall never forget it: "The greatest professionals are hopelessly amateurs in that they get thrilled and excited when confronted with music. They're like little children. You can no more be a professional musician than you can be a professional human being, professional Christian or a professional lover."

Skill can be refined, but it must be put into submission to the all-consuming desire to know God, my fellowman, and to share, to weep, to laugh and to go on pilgrimages with people I love. If I am skilled in one area such as singing or speaking, it in no way relieves me of the responsibility of being the most complete servant I can be.

Loving is for everybody. Faith is for everybody. Witnessing is for everybody. The person who does not wonder at the love of God and hurt when his brother hurts is limited indeed. I feel the singer who believes he has absolved himself from all responsibility of transmitting God's love when he's finished his concert, deprives himself of the experience of giving and receiving the healing, restoring, redeeming feedback that comes only from interaction with others.

We have just a few minutes of intermission left and while we're standing here in the breeze, let me confide in you that one of my deepest concerns regards the matter of manipulation of emotions.

I know that human beings have only one set of mechanisms with which to respond to everything. There is nothing wrong with emotion, but I am very afraid of too much emotion when a response is called for in a religious gathering. Partly as a result of my heritage, partly as a result of my sense of proportion and balance, and partly as a result of some healthy input from my wife, I am leery of some of the hyper-emotionalism that is rampant in evangelical religious gatherings.

I realize that as a musician, particularly as a singer, I hold in my hand a tool that has immense potential for reaching and manipulating the emotions of people. Music can bring folks to tears. Music can incite anger, happiness, regret, remorseful memory, pleasant recollection. It also can bring a person to a point of considerable vulnerability. I must be careful about that, for I strongly believe that the emotions will fail you when a push becomes a shove. I mean that emotions do not provide very stable ground for decision-making. Consequently, the only faculty that I can really depend on in decision-making is the *will*. It is not the harmonizing of my emotions and God's emotions, nor my reason and God's reason, but my will and God's will that is crucial. My will is not denied in that decision but rather is *exercised* in that decision. My will makes a choice—to come into harmony with what I know of God's will.

It seems almost contradictory to use a musical medium that is so emotion-oriented to try and stimulate a decision based on a response of the will. However, this is the challenge I have set for myself. To help me in my task I have chosen to use such devices as allegory where one can be somewhat removed from a situation and therefore less emotionally involved.

I have made my invitations short and crisp. I have stressed in most places where I have sung the need to go beyond the feelings of tears into the domain of the will. I would like to be able to count the times I have said to young people, "Your reason and your emotions will fail you. Your will is the only thing you can depend on to really make a decision—a choice for God."

Commitment is not feeling you would like to do something. Commitment is not a promise and a tear. The conscious examination of risk considering all the issues, determining to make a specific choice and providing for yourself the wherewithal to follow through on the choice you have made—that is commitment. That means providing time, resources, thought-energy, money, whatever is necessary. If we can somehow communicate these ideas then I think we will make tremendous strides toward a better understanding of what Jesus wants of his disciples.

Well, it's time to go on. They're dimming the houselights and they expect the singer to come walking on stage and touch those keys again.

Thanks for this talk. I needed it. I'll feel better about performing now that you know where I stand on these things. Come on, we'd better go inside. It's time to sing.

8

You Can't Go Back

You can't go back to the music of yesterday.
You gotta stop hiding, you got to stop running
    away.
Yesterday's drumbeat isn't gonna help you now.
You've got to find a new beat to march to,
You've got to make tomorrow work somehow.

The houselights are down and we've begun the second half of the program. I have begun to sing a song that troubles some people in my audience; perhaps they do not realize that these lyrics were never intended to refer literally to music. Rather, I am speaking metaphorically of the need for change. This song always reminds me of my wife—a restless, exploring, questioning person.

Jane is such a vital part of what I do that I encourage people to speak of the music as *our* ministry. I could tell you how Jane feels about this or that, but I would prefer to let her talk to you herself.

"I am often weary because I cannot keep from racing

my mind—my head seems to have an independent life that compulsively weasels through ideas and concepts. Like my mother, I love to make long lists of all the questions one may ask on any subject; unlike her, I am never at peace with the answers. Consider this aspect of my personality in relationship to Ken's rebellion—that's where our communication met during that period when Ken was struggling against Christianity. It wasn't that I was so tactful and knew just the right things to say, but simply that the questions he was asking did not affront me. For me, asking questions was natural and healthy, something I had been made to feel comfortable doing as a Christian.

"I guess one of the most overwhelming experiences of my life was talking to my daddy once about my fear as a Christian regarding doubt. I don't remember how I asked him about it, but I recall daddy saying, 'You start inside a magic circle of the Lord's care and love for you. You go out as far as you want. You go and you keep going, and keep going and keep going wherever there is honest doubt. And you keep questioning with the comfortable assumption that no matter how far you run from the middle, the circle is drawn beyond that.' I have followed that advice (sometimes further than Daddy would have guessed) without any more fear of lostness.

"Ken was running from an environment which he believed kept him from asking the very questions I had always had the freedom to ask. He knew his doubt was honest. More than he realized, he was open to the Lord's

94

response to those questions. We worked through the whole list of 'yes, buts,' always coming back to the basic need to *trust* that God was about his business, and Ken was included in his plans.

"Since that early beginning, the key to our joy has been a yearning to grow spiritually together. When we have to struggle over something, we try to wring every spiritual benefit out of that hard time. Later we can rejoice, knowing it has been worth it all. I cannot relate to persons who have met no dragons to slay along the route of discipleship.

"Now, given Ken's and my own training and experience as teacher and therapist, we have a 'language' with which we can express what is happening to us. We can use therapeutic terms when we run out of religious ones. This is a grand advantage when one needs to communicate what is happening inside.

"There is also a tremendous release in finding a way to share nonverbal experience. We indulge a great deal in analogies, symbols, and 'bent words.' The focus on communication has resulted in growth for us and for our friends. Ken and I are convinced that the Word speaks in the dialogue of the Christian community, even in its smallest and most intimate expression, the marriage of two believers.

"There is no way I would change the way things are. I married Ken because I love him. I don't care if he's performing, as he's doing now, or what, my concern is that whatever it is, it's helping people to crystallize where their turmoil is. Then, when they can speak it,

95

if only to themselves, they are freer and are able to move in a new direction.

"I don't know what I'm planning for my own future. My primary reason for going to seminary now is because of my own involvement in what Ken is doing. In order to bring a disciplined theological perspective to his material, I want to be better informed. But what I do with my life apart from his ministry is also important.

"I am on the Master of Divinity degree program at Union Theological Seminary, and I will finish that program if the material along the way is what we need to take. But, what I have done is choose the courses that seemed at the moment most needed by Ken and me. I am going to the seminary for 'both of us.'

"It has been exciting and challenging to me to attend Union Seminary. I have found hosts of different kinds of pilgrims who have great vitality in their faith, an urgency in their feelings to respond and to commit themselves to God. I have also discovered reasons for valuing my particular religious heritage. I have made countless choices—what to hold on to, what to discard.

"I am incubating some personal ambitions as well. I have been trained as a teacher. I love being in the classroom and I have a real sense of victory there—a real sense of being allowed to use gifts that a lot of the time I don't use. I would like someday to use professionally what I'm doing in the seminary. I dream of a time when Ken and I can work jointly with groups, perhaps at conferences or retreats. That is why I am focusing on biblical studies.

"Attending school is taxing, not only on me, but on the whole family. I feel very happy and comfortable with Ken's and my understanding at this point. We are cooperating in the life we are making. There are times when both of us must give to the other—make each other's concern at the moment a priority.

"There are times when Ken's schedule takes priority for us, not because the things he's doing are more valuable to us, but because his time is tightly structured by the particular demands of his kind of work. I feel it's the ideal way for men and women to work together, a real give and take on priorities.

"Ken's tremendous amount of traveling and being away from home have been hard for me. With me going to seminary in New York, I see him only about three days a week. I fantasize going up to him and saying, 'Ken, I can't stand it. I don't like you being gone this much. I married you with the assumption that I would be with you all the time.'

"The first seven years of our marriage we were together constantly. We worked together two years in Indiana. We went back to graduate school and took the same courses. We were together day and night. I liked that. Ken liked that. Suddenly it wasn't that way and I remember thinking, 'I can't stand this. You've got to quit.' But what he is doing I want him to do. I don't want him to stop. So I don't ask.

97

"There were some things about Ken's traveling that I really had to struggle with. I had to learn to prepare balanced meals and keep regular sleeping hours when he was gone. I had to cope with going places and being involved in church life by myself rather than the 'two of us.' What do you do socially when you're a single woman? Everyone knows that's a problem in our society. Where does the single woman go—particularly when she cannot have the advantages of the divorced woman or the widow? Always being the one woman at the party without the husband there was something I had to work through.

"There were other adjustments along the way. Persons in my own family are handicapped, so Ken's blindness was not a novel experience. I already knew the wisdom of turning kitchen knives pointed ends down in the dish drainer, setting hot irons out of reach, keeping drawers and cabinets organized. I change room arrangements when I wish, but I remember to tell Ken about the new locations. I sew color labels in his clothes and pack his suitcases according to routine. I almost never remember that I am doing things in such and such a way because of his handicap. It has become automatic.

"Yet, I do not feel as comfortable and blithe and easy with Ken's blindness as some have supposed. It does, occasionally, cause self-consciousness on my part when I think of the habits Ken has had to fight all the years I've known him—I'm referring to the habits typical of blind people such as squinting and rubbing the eyes, and head movements. These habits have always

been annoying to me—annoying because they embar-
rass me personally, because Ken does them, and because
I am married to him. Like most people, I think I want
image. I want it to be an honest one but I still want that
sense of rapport that makes me feel confident of myself.

"Having to come to terms with what is feminine in
the role I have has caused me to make some major
adjustments in my own personality. What is it to be a
woman who does all the bill paying, who takes care of
all the money, who always drives the car, who makes
sure the doors are locked at night, who is responsible
for the home? I've even learned to be a pretty fair house
painter! You see, in most homes, these things are the
male roles. I've had to cope with that and come to terms
with what makes me feel feminine, what makes me feel
like a woman.

"I think the thing that does characterize our relationship, and always has, is that blindness is not a larger
issue than any of the other limitations that people always
struggle with in a relationship. It's the same annoyance
that somebody else feels whose husband spends too
much on cigarettes. It's the annoyance another person
feels because her husband works to hard, travels too
much. It's the annoyance somebody feels when the husband screams at the kids. It's the little things you cope
with that you deal with. Ken's blindness is no larger
than that to us. Besides, I have a bonus benefit: I get to
select his entire wardrobe!

"We maximize the fun of being together when he is
at home. We're addicted to 'Star Trek' reruns, late

dinners, and washing dishes together. We read by the hour. I hate for the phone to ring, so we turn it off when we need to be alone.

"Like most couples, we plan a dream house. Ours is contemporary. It has a soaking tub, sunrooms, skylights, fireplaces, plants, a combination kitchen and living area—no wasted space, but room for company. There must be carpeting everywhere, since we all go barefoot. We argue about what items are unnecessary luxuries.

"We are seriously considering the possibility of planning a home that would be a multiple family community for other people in traveling ministry.

"Now, where we build this house is something Ken and I don't know at the present. We're both crazy about the Northeast and we feel at home here. What intrigues us and draws us here, what makes us feel comfortable is the infinite variety. We like to get on the subway and see the faces that are every color; see the clothes of every style; hear all the different languages; smell all the different smells. There's a pungent feel here, a briskness in the way people act, a frankness that can be rude but that's there right in front of you. You can deal with it the way it comes. I like the lack of formality.

"We belong to a small church. We couldn't feel comfortable in a large church with a large staff where it is so easy to lose intimacy and an awareness of each person's gift to the Body.

"Ken and I agonize about the comforts that we do have in a world with inequality. We agonize over whether we ought to be giving more to missions,

100

whether we should be more politically active than we are.

"This past fall we joined a political party. We felt the need to say, 'We want to take a stand. We learned that for us noncommitment is noninvolvement. It is where our money can go, where our voice can be heard! Until now we've been very naïve about this.

"I believe in new beginnings, new learning experiences—these will always have to be a part of our lives. It's the feeling of, 'Today there's a little way in which I'll stretch these muscles and start to grow.'

"We feel God is with us, to empower and to act through us. I think that means taking those half-steps, assuming that when you get half-way, then God empowers you to go the rest of the way.

"Sometimes I overdo spiritual restlessness. I want to learn to be more comfortable with myself; to live within my limitations and say, 'God sees me as OK today,' without giving up my need to grow and be different. This is a hard thing for me. I think it ought to be hard. What motivates me unless I'm restless and dissatisfied with what I am?

"On the other hand, there's something very healthy about being 'at home' at this moment knowing, 'It's all right to be what I am right now.' Ken and I are ministering to one another to meet at that place of 'all right.'

"It's sad, in a way, but Ken is always some place else from where his audience is. Most people are still dealing with Ken through the music they have available to them. What they're really listening to is music he wrote

two years ago. I guess that's why in many of his concerts disappointed people will say, 'Oh, he didn't do
such and such' . . . because that's where they are relating
to him.

"But Ken cannot go back to the music of yesterday.
He cannot go back to yesterday's lessons. He has to
deal with where he is now. That's what makes Ken's
music so fresh and alive. I think his music has to be this
way. This is not just for Ken, but for the thousands who
sit and hear him play and sing about life with God as he
is applying it in the now."

Jane is truly a unique person. I believe that one of her
most unique qualities is her perception, her constant
awareness that yesterday's music is stale and a rather
unhealthy tune to sing when today's music needs all the
instruments and attention we can give it. She keeps me
remembering that there may be a "new beat to march
to." And, oh yes, we have some progress to make between yesterday and tomorrow.

This next piece is about a journey. And so, a little
traveling music, if you please!

9

~~~~~~~~~~~~~~~ *Long, Long Journey*

> I'm goin' away on a long, long journey.
> I don't know where the road will end.
> I'm goin' away on a long, long journey.
> One thing I know is that I'll need a friend.

As we begin, I want to sing you a song that is a story. The story is partly my story and partly yours, partly that of hundreds of people to whom I've talked in the last several years. The story draws its material from the writings of some authors who have become heroes to me.

We've read almost all of the works of C. S. Lewis, *Lord of the Rings* trilogy by J. R. R. Tolkien. We've read books by Charles Williams, George McDonald and many others. Jane and I are both crazy about adult fantasy and if you want to get a good feeling for the kind of literature that really rings my bells, read C. S. Lewis's, *The Great Divorce*, one of the most magnificent books I've ever read.

All these books I've mentioned have in common the use of fantasy and allegory. I've taken up this interest and I've become a bit of a storyteller myself. So, the song-story that I will sing to you now is partly my story, but it is perhaps a universal story also. Maybe it's the story of millions of Christians all over the world who are wrestling with "what it is" and "what it means" to be a Christian and to follow Christ. You'll find autobiography here and maybe when I finish you'll want to tell your own story.

It happened at the beginning of my journey that I stood upon a mountain looking and looking over a vast land. There were villages, hills, towns, cities, monumental towers, rivers, large mountains, deep volcanoes, craggy rock cliffs, beautiful green forests and a great, long road that ran through the middle of the land.

I surveyed and I saw there by the edge of the Dark Sea, which was on the extreme outer edge of the land, what looked like a community. No sooner did I see it than suddenly I found myself there at the edge of the Dark Sea.

I look back in retrospect now, and I see that the sea was black and murky and there was rising from it a great mist and we all breathed the mist. In the mist was our life. We did not know that the mist kept our hands from feeling and our feet from being able to walk and our eyes from being able to see and our ears from being able to hear, our minds from perceiving and our hearts from understanding. We did not know that there was any other way to live than groveling in the dust and the dirt and the mud by the edge of the sea.

We even sang about it in our folk songs:

> Oh, the mist that rises from the sea,
> Oh, the mist that rises from the sea.
> It is true and it is sound that our source
>   of life is found
> In the mist that rises from the sea.

And so there we remained. We touched, but did not really feel. We did not hear the sounds of the forest and the breeze and the rain.

Then on a day one came among us who was later to be called One-With-Us. One called in a clarion voice, not loud but strong, "To anyone who will follow me, I will give the gift of hearing and seeing and understanding and touching and walking and running and breathing. Breathing not this mist that rises from the sea, but the air that comes down from the Great Mountain in the center of the land where the King of all these parts dwells."

Most of us could not hear. Our ears were deaf. But, for a few who heard the call in the dim recesses of our groggy, numbed intelligence, there was a response. Something in the call made us want to come, made us want to follow.

And so, we crawled after our leader. We told One-With-Us, "Yes, we *will* follow you. Wherever you take us we'll follow you."

So, the journey began there at the edge of the Dark Sea. "First," he said, "you must learn to breathe the air that comes down from the mountain. You must stop

105

breathing the mist that rises from the sea, for in the mist is poison and danger."

One-With-Us taught us how to stand up and look with heads raised toward the mountains and deeply breathe that air so clear, so clean, so bright, so pure. The air was so clear it hurt our lungs! But, we felt life surging through our bodies. We felt muscles begin to work that had never worked before. We felt the exhilaration of a spring morning. We felt at that moment as if all of life had suddenly come bursting in upon us.

"What else could there be?" we cried. "This is ecstasy! There is no more to be said."

"No, my children," said One-With-Us, "there is the road that stretches on and on and on and on to the Mountain. Remember I will always be with you, but beware of the villages that lie along the side of the road for there is value *and* danger in those villages. As long as you walk through them and do not stop to remain in them, they will help you. However, if you stop there, you will be hurt and your journey will be impeded."

> In the growing is the rising,
> In the growing is the falling,
> In the growing is the holding,
> In the growing is the letting go.
>
> In the growing is the leaping,
> In the growing is the stumbling,
> In the growing is the joining,
> In the growing is the saying, 'No.'

106

In the growing is the running free,
In the growing shackles there must be,
In the growing is the fearing,
In the growing is the trusting,
In the growing is the doubting,
In the growing is the saying, 'No.'

So the road began, each day the same—practice in breathing, practice in walking, instructions from One-With-Us. Practice in touching, practice in hearing. Each day a new thing to see, a new thing to hear, a new way to have our perceptions expanded.

Oh, such a long road this is! What craggy cliffs and rocks fall in our path. How barren sometimes these trees seem to be. Long days and not enough sleep. Breathing, walking, touching, seeing, hearing, learning—and aching, too, for with the coming of life always comes pain.

What's this? What's this coming up on the road here? A village? It is a village indeed, a pleasant place, warm, with a warm climate. It is a beautiful place—Glowington. Beaches, sand, surf, sea, smiles, and there is much kissing and embracing everywhere.

In the center of the town is the Glowington Inn and the proprietor comes out on the road and sings to us a song:

Come, good children, it's inspirational,
Don't you want to take a hand?
Come, good children, it's sensational,
Don't you know the feeling's grand?

> Come, good children, come make the music.
> You can do it if you try.
> Welcome, children, to the Glowington Inn
> Where living is a natural high.

It was a beautiful song and captivating. It drew us to the doorway of the inn. We looked in and some of us went into the inn to sit for just awhile. And the feelings, oh, the feelings—the smiles, the warmth, the feeling of love for each other. Everybody loves everyone else. Everybody is happy.

And so we sat there in the Glowington Inn, reveling in the joy of our feelings. We sat and sat and sat for a long time and day followed day, sun followed sun and we noticed that our legs began to be numb. We noticed, some of us, that as we breathed the air in Glowington there was a touch of the old familiar fragrance of the mist that rises from . . .

Then, there was a knock at the door, and there stood One-With-Us half-smiling and half-frowning. It was an ambivalent look, showing reluctance to remove us from that inn but knew that we had to go.

"Come, children. There is a place for glowing, but true glowing is to be found only on the road. You cannot remain here in the Glowington Inn, for as I told you, there are dangers here. Come follow the road with me and let's walk."

Many of our number stayed. Some of us came resentfully. Some of us came gladly. All of us came with pain for when you have been in Glowington and you know you have to leave, you know that there is something you may never find again. Sadder but wiser? Maybe.

On down the road we went and the routine was the same—new things to learn, new places to walk, new ways to experiment and explore with the parts of our bodies that we had never known before. Things like new ways for the head to turn and the hands to grasp and the legs to run. There were new things to sense and perceive.

But, here was another town! It was a good town, a town full of beautiful, elegant, aesthetically satisfying buildings. The streets were laid out in geometric patterns. The arts flourished here. This was Knowington.

Two places we saw in the town. The first was a house that lay at the edge of the town. It was called the House of Square and within the House of Square were all sorts of boxes, each one having answers to questions. All that one needed to do was go to the proprietor of the House of Square and say, "I have a question." He would look through his boxes until he found the answer. The answer would be recorded on a small slip of paper and the answer would usually be one or two or three phrases—neat, clean, authoritative.

Usually these answers came from what he called a prooftext and I suspect sometimes from a misinterpretation of a prooftext! One- or two-sentence answers to all the questions. If a question had no answer in the House of Square, then the question was irrelevant.

Now, for some of our number the House of Square was too naïve so they went on. They went on through the town to the Knowington Tower, down Analysis Street, Synthesis Street, Categorization Street.

They began to climb. New knowledge with each step. And when they reached the top of the tower there sat the Knowers, despising most of the other Growers, especially the Glowers. Before them on the table was a flower.

"See," they said, "we have analyzed this flower, we know all there is to know about it and we have discovered the truth."

While they sat there reveling in the knowledge of the flower, there came a knock at the door. It was One-With-Us. One held in hand a flower saying: "See, this is a mystery beyond all your knowing."

"Children, I did not mean for you to stay here. There is a place for knowing, but knowing has its place only on the road. Knowing and glowing will all fit together on the road, for on the road proportion, balance, variety, combination—all these things will come together."

Some of the number decided to remain in the Knowington Tower and some remained in the House of Square, but for those few of us who walked down the road there was a curious sense of mindlessness. When you think you know and you discover that you don't know, it leaves a void for awhile.

On down the road we went and as we walked we saw the lights and the smoke of a great city. This was perhaps the largest city in all the land. It was a huge industrial complex, full of factories, moving buses, cars, trains, noise, smoke, high-rise apartments. This was Strivington.

At the very center of Strivington was the great complex that made up Strivington Industries. The foreman was old Master Guilt and for those of our number who felt the desperate need to work and to do good and to produce, the Strivington Industries always had an open door.

One came into the Strivington Industries to work for old Master Guilt and one was immediately put to a task—the more tasks the better. There was no limit to the hours, no labor laws, no labor unions—just work, work, work. The longer you wanted to work the more it pleased old Master Guilt.

And he whipped his workers. He whipped them hard to make them work and the harder they worked to avoid the whip, the harder he whipped them to make them work. As they continued to labor in that hot, dusty place of noise and confusion all around them, their bodies began to shrink under the weight of the whipping and the weight of the work until they were only a small shadow of themselves.

One-With-Us came on a day knocking at the door of Strivington Industries, saying to his children, "My children, you have been made only a fraction of what you once were by this old Master Guilt whose breeding and growing are from the sea. The whip is made of cords taken from reeds grown by the edge of the sea. His nostrils are full of the mist of the sea and in his blood is water from the Dark Sea. Do not follow or work for this one. Do not be controlled. Come out in the fields and let's fly a kite and run and play and dance." Some of them came out.

In the fields outside of Strivington, we experienced perhaps the greatest sense of freedom that we had ever had on the road.

"I don't have to," was the cry.

"I am not forced to," one said.

"I can do as I please," said someone else.

"Guilt has no dominion over me," said another.

"Come," said One-With-Us, in the midst of all the reveling, "we have a road to walk. You're not there yet, children."

So, for those of us who were willing to come One took us on down the road through the rocks and the trees, the underbrush, through the dry places where the sun beat down on our heads and we wanted water, through the oases, and then we saw the lights of a town before us.

We were all tired and as we approached the town we heard a great clamor and commotion for this was Talkington. And there in the Talkington square you could hear all manner of conversations.

There were the conversations in large, round, comfortable words—great debaters holding forth for hours to convince us all of their philosophy. There were the conversations in short, earthy natural phrases: "It's real, man. It's honest." But all there found its expression in conversation—talk, talk, talk. The longer we stood in the Talkington square and talked, learned new words, learned how to modulate our voices, the more numb became our feet and the colder our hands became. We realized we were becoming rooted to the ground on which we stood.

One by one our leader approached us again. "You are talking too much and there is a place for talking. But you can learn the right words to say only on the road. And there is a place for doing and talking and knowing and glowing—but all on the road. Will you follow me?"

For those of us who followed and walked slowly out of the Talkington square and onto the road again, there was an immense silence, a silence so imposing you could feel it all around you. There is nothing left to say. There is only the road. Yet, there *are* things to be said and they *will* be found. We *will* say them. The time will be right and the place will be for saying and the proportion and the balance will be perfect.

Tired pilgrims. Weary pilgrims. Such a long road it's been! And here's a village, so quiet, so sleepy, so comfortable, with little houses all in a row, all with great bay windows facing the Great Mountain. In each bay window sat a traveler in a chair for this was Waitington.

The conversation ran something like this:

"Won't it be delicious to sit in the palace of the King and admire and adore him?"

"Won't it be wonderful when the day finally comes that we are relieved from this awful, long road?"

As they talked in muffled voices, they looked through their bay windows, rooted to their chairs, their hands growing numb, their minds becoming dull and their eyes slowly closing as if in sleep.

"No, no," came the clarion cry in the middle of the street. "No, no, there is no waiting to be done. There is a place for waiting, but not here. You will wait upon *me*, but you must *walk* and wait. Waiting and walking and talking and doing and knowing and glowing— they're all a part of the road."

Some of the pilgrims got up from their lethargic chairs and walked, as if on half-paralyzed legs, back to the main road.

"Follow me," One said, at this point literally dancing.

We walked and walked and walked and walked, it seemed, for hours, our walking stretching on into days. We came to the edge of a hill overlooking something and there he stood weeping on the edge of the hill. We saw before us—the Dark Sea.

"But, One-With-Us," we cried, "you've led us all the way around and we're no further than we were before."

"Oh, yes, children, for in the walking you've learned about the dangers of the towns. Your feet have learned to walk and run and dance and skip. Your hands have learned to grasp and heal and mend and mold. Your eyes have learned to see the differences between real and unreal. Your hearts have learned to understand. Your minds can think. You know, and you know the place of knowing and glowing and doing and talking and waiting.

"Now I bring you to this Dark Sea because it is your

task before your life is finished, to come to those thousands of your kindred. Bring them to my road and nurture them as they walk the sometimes hurting, sometimes joyful paths that I will set before them. Bring them to my road and walk along beside them, 'round and 'round and 'round the circle, for it is a circle. All the way around the land goes the road in a circle and we come back and back and back to the same places— Strivington again, Glowington again, Knowington again. But this time you will know and you will advise. You cannot take the trial for them, but you can walk them through it. You can help them understand. You must remold and remake and renew and refresh this dark, dismal place at the edge of the sea so that there is no rubbish left. No broken, hopeless bodies. No paralyzed, unhearing, unseeing children of mine. And when your work is done then I shall bring you to the Mountain."

As we looked across the Dark Sea we saw there, reflected in the glow of the morning sun, the immense palace where the King lived. And there around the palace, dancing, running, seemingly several stories tall— the people, the real people bathed in light, full of joy and expectation, crowding around to hear the words of the King. They were bending low before him, dancing on clouds, running through fields, climbing in trees, looking up joyfully at the light, clapping their hands for sheer ecstasy.

"That will be your home, children, a whole eternity to grow in. So, will you respond to my challenge? Will you who are learning to see and to hear and to become, work here at the edge of the sea? And when your work is over I will take you across this Sea of Death to a new home."

Many turned back. But some put their hands to the task, their feet walking through the mire, their eyes always on the lookout for some*one* or some*thing* to be redeemed, their ears listening to the groans and the cries and the ache of the edge-of-the-sea world, their hearts hurting, reaching, their minds understanding, planning, organizing. There is a place for glowing and knowing and talking and doing and waiting.

So, I find myself sometimes at the edge of the sea, working. Sometimes back in Strivington or Glowington or Knowington, for the road is a circle, as he said. Always there is the knowledge that though it may hurt and though it may be a difficult road, One-With-Us is beside me walking the way with me.

Where will the road end? I know that it will end beyond the Sea of Death in the mountains. What are the intermediate places on the road? I don't know. There are places I've not seen yet. I do know that:

> I'm bound away on a long, long journey
> I'll be walking through the darkness of the
>   night.
> I'm bound away on a long, long journey.
> I'm bound away to find the light.
> I'm bound away on a long, long journey.
> The road will be long, I will not find much rest.

I'm bound away on a long, long journey.
The answer to a riddle is my quest.

And the riddle:

> Finding leads to losing,
> Losing lets you find,
> Dying leads to living
> And life leaves death behind.
>
> Losing leads to finding,
> That's all that one can say.
> No pilgrim will find life
> Another way.

10

~~~~~~~~~~~~~~~~~~~~~~~~~~~ *Come with Me,*
Fly with Me

Come with me, walk with me,
Run with me, fly with me.
We will roam the Father's land
Together.

As I sit here trying to sing to you my song about
"coming with me and flying with me," it occurs to me
that I divide my world in two. There is At Home and
there is Not-At-Home. I suppose this is normal for most
people, although I wonder if most people have the
sense of security, peace, calm and delicious enjoyment
that I have at home.

Let's look at At Home first. At the time of this writing, my son, Aaron, my wife, Jane, and I are living in
an upstairs apartment, part of a two-family house in
Upper Montclair, New Jersey.

How did we get there? Well, after I resigned my
music therapy position, I liked my location so well I

decided to stay. We could actually live in a central location such as Chicago, Kansas City, or on the East Coast, Atlanta. However, I am so attached to the New York Metropolitan area that at the moment I don't want to leave it.

The house we live in is an old house, maybe sixty or seventy years old. It feels old. It has high ceilings and the rooms feel big. There is a lot of space and the stairways echo. There is a front hall that has a long stairway and a high ceiling and I would like to put an organ there someday. There is a grand echo in that place and it smells like an old church.

We have a living room on the floor of which there is now a very thick comfortable green rug. I love to lie on that rug and listen to music or listen to the breeze outside the window or just vegetate.

Off the living room is a dining room and it is furnished with a butcher-block table and six chairs. Off the dining room is a beautiful sun porch with windows on three sides. This is my office. This is also the room where most of the stereo equipment is located. I make no bones about it—I am a stereo nut! If it were not for the care that my wife takes to remind me of our necessary expenses, I think I would go and purchase a new set of speakers every week and probably run us flat into bankruptcy!

I am trying to decide, as I write this, what my favorite room is in the house. I find I cannot, for each of the rooms has its own personality. The living room with its glass-top coffee table, plants in the artificial fireplace, thick green carpet, stereo speakers and no echo—this room is a quiet place.

The sun porch is a "happening" place. Everything happens there! Since the stereo and the old couch are there (the new couch is in the living room!) most of the family snacking is done in the sun room. At least three times out of four when I come home from a trip, the beneath-the-cushions part of the couch is scattered with cracker crumbs, popsicle sticks—by you-know-who! I'll talk about Aaron later.

The kitchen is one of those old kitchens that is large and you walk a mile to get from one end to the other. My favorite part of the kitchen is the portion of the counter where the coffee pot stands. I make the coffee at my house and I maintain almost exclusive rights on coffee-making. I don't know why I enjoy that part of my existence so much. I just blame it on my Dutch blood.

I also fix a rather good breakfast. I'm a decent omelette chef, although I have been told on many occasions that there is at least half as much salt on the stove as in the pan and Jane always wonders why there are little pieces of grated cheese on the floor. But, if you can live with those minor problems, I fix a pretty good omelette. I always wake up hungry so I enjoy eating a hearty breakfast.

Behind our bedroom, which is off the kitchen, there's another sun porch. My sun porch, being on the second story, is really up in the treetops and it is quite possible to go there in the morning with a cup of coffee and some things to think about and chatter back at the squirrels who are perhaps no more than ten feet away from my window.

I feel close to my house. I love its walls and its old-fashioned doorknobs. I love the way the doors bang. I love the sounds in my house. The little ways it squeaks when the wind blows. It's a remarkably well-put-together house. It's solid. Of course, I don't notice that the paint is beginning to fall off on the outside.

In my house there live two outrageously beautiful people and two Abyssinian cats—Aslan and Galadrill. We had a silver Persian once named Gandalf. We stole these names from J. R. R. Tolkien and C. S. Lewis. (I'm going to get you to read those books if it's the last thing I do!). The late Satin Psyche was named from C. S. Lewis's novel.

There is no way I can describe to you my wife, Jane. I could tell you that she is a physically attractive person. I could tell you that she is fairly tall and slender. I could tell you that she has a sense of style. But, I think what means more to me than all of those things is that my wife is not only my house companion, my lover, but she is my very best friend.

We have been very fortunate to be the best friends of one another. Before we were ever engaged we fought all the battles best friends have to fight, coming to know each other, expecting things of each other, making demands on each other. After the engagement was settled, the battles stopped. Although we have not agreed on everything, and though we have had differing opinions on many things, there has never been a climate of fighting.

Jane is also my best critic. She is never satisfied. I think that is a chronic characteristic of her personality— never satisfied with anything but the best. Then, when we have achieved what we think is the best, we realize it is second best and we must go further.

I am convinced that without Jane's continual help, loving criticism and support, I would never have the kind of ministry that I have now. I am convinced, also, that I would be content with simplistic answers to many of my questions. I probably would never have been willing to deal with the chameleon aspect of my personality.

She and I complement each other very well, I think. I can't tell you the number of times our conversations together have stimulated me, challenged my mind, made me want to be more than I am. Understand me, now, I am not trying to make Jane perfect. Jane has her limitations, too. I feel that one of the ways I complement my wife is in the stability I can provide for her.

My wife possesses a master's degree in music. Not long ago she became dissatisfied with her condition; that is, a "once" teacher not working, tending to child. Not wanting to go back into music, she enrolled in Union Theological Seminary where she is now working on a Master of Divinity. I can see in her work the desire never to be satisfied with the status quo. The desire always to know, to talk it out, to discover, to discuss and if not to solve, at least to bring up every conceivable problem that could arise.

Jane is an extremely sensitive person and I have particularly appreciated her sensitivity to many aspects of my ministry. We spoke earlier about Christian artists who get trapped in the commercial, superpublicity game. I must admit that Jane has been the primary force in helping me to maintain my faith in the ministry as it is now conducted.

I am a naturally acquisitive person. Jane balances that for me very well with her fear of having too much money and not knowing what to do with it. We're not very good about managing money. I suppose we should be making investments, have a creditable savings account, be paying into a retirement plan, but as of this moment we have done very little investing for the future. Right now, money is for helping friends, giving to a worthy cause, taking parents out to dinner, going to Europe, green rugs and books.

How does one talk about one's wife? How can I make you feel what I feel for her? How can I help you understand what it's like to have a wife who is your best friend, the most exciting mind that you know, the least threatening person in your existence? How can I help you to grasp the depth of my gratitude to her for what she has given and what she has been to me? I guess there's no way. You'll just have to imagine.

At the time of this writing, Aaron is nine years old. I jokingly say he is going on thirteen! Aaron is a talker, he's good with words and has a huge vocabulary. He is a playful, enthusiastic, happy child who loves to be with adults and enter into their conversations. Although he hates to practice, he's taking piano lessons. His attitude about piano may change. Whether he's a pianist or not will certainly be his own decision. He's particularly interested in projects that require other people's assistance, à la Tom Sawyer.

And Aaron loves to play! Always playing a practical joke or a game. How many times a day do I hear these words, "Dad, wanna play games?" or "Dad, pretend that you are a . . ." or "Who's for Chinese checkers?"

One of our favorite times together is story time. Sometimes the stories are told lying on the bed just before tucking-in time. Sometimes they are told from the top of a tree in the park a few blocks away. That's right, we climb trees together! You should see the looks I get. I'm glad *I* can't!

I like the way Aaron is growing up. Our philosophy has always been that we are training Aaron for the kind of adult we want him to be. I wouldn't say that he is the quietest, most disciplined, most retiring child I've ever seen. I have some friends who would concur with that and would take it even further. But Aaron is a child who loves life, who loves people and opens himself to them. He enjoys experiencing and learning. There is a sense of life when you are around Aaron. I like to pick up on that. He refreshes me and he makes me know that living is worthwhile. He makes me know that living is fun and free and flying and crazy.

And when I've told that story he knows it's time for bed. He says, "Good night, dad," hugs me tight and I know I have a son who loves me. Aaron knows of my love, too.

There's a good three-way love thing going at our house. We talk about it a lot. We say many times a day, "I love you," for I have discovered that to say the words together leaves many doors open. It's hard to say, "I love you," when you're bearing a grudge. Therefore, we like to say it.

I love the times when friends come and we sit around the table with candles lit, talking, and listening to music, but mostly talking. We do a lot of talking. We sometimes criticize ourselves for not being very entertaining with our friends. They come over and we just talk— but they keep coming, and they keep wanting to come. So, maybe they keep wanting to talk.

My Not-At-Home world consists of airports, planes, motels, churches, high school auditoriums, city streets and it seems I am always running. I never get away from the sense of running. Dash to the airport in a taxi. Run to the ticket counter. "What seat do you want, Mr. Medema?"

I must say that although I almost always travel alone, I never really feel very much alone. I have never ridden with any airline that has not been extremely helpful. There are always agents to bring me from the counter to the gate, from the gate onto the plane and someone always brings me from the plane to the cab.

I really would like to compliment the airline personnel with whom I have flown for doing a spectacular job of not only escorting me from place to place, but sensing my needs. I have spent many long hours in airports waiting for the next flight, usually late at night. I prefer to leave after an evening concert and get home rather than spend an extra night away. So, while I'm sitting in some airport at 3:00 A.M. in the morning in Dallas, Chicago or Atlanta, the agent will come to me and say, "Need a cup of coffee? How about something to eat? You look like you might need something to eat."

Thank you, all of you—Braniff, United, Delta, American, Allegheny, and all the rest—thank you for your help.

Get off the plane. Meet the music director.

"Yes, Ken, you'll have about forty-five minutes in the evening service tonight. You'll have the whole evening tomorrow."

Begin to pick up the vibes. On the way to the motel I ask questions about the church.

"How long has your church been here? Where are your areas of ministry? Who do you think will be at this concert? What kinds of music have your people heard before? What about this concert in the high school auditorium? Do you expect lots of people from around the community to come? Do you think many of them are not Christians? How shall I direct the evening?"

Check into the motel. Find the room and memorize the path between the room and restaurant. Oh, the restaurant! Tomorrow morning I can have a cheese omelette! I love to have cheese omelettes when I'm on the road. Some restaurants use American cheese; some restaurants use Cheddar cheese—but a cheese omelette is always a good thing so be sure you have the pathway to the restaurant memorized.

Run to the church. Meet the minister. Ask questions. Catch vibrations.

"Some young person would like to talk to you."

"Yes, Ken, I saw you in Connecticut three years ago," or "You came to my college last year," or "I wrote you a letter three months ago and you forgot to answer."

"I know," I say. "That happens more often than I'd like. I'm doing better, though. Write me again."

Time for the concert. Where are we going this time? I may not know until the last thirty seconds before I sit down to play. All the preparation of years of piano study, voice work, reading, thinking, praying, experiencing, agonizing, enjoying, relating—it all comes together now and the question is, "What happens tonight?"

Back to the motel for coffee after the concert. Let's talk about it.

"What did you think? No, I don't mean did you enjoy it. I mean, where do we go tomorrow? What did I not say that has to be said? What were the facial expressions? How were people responding? Do you think allegory is the right kind of medium for your church? Do you think the people who come to the high school auditorium tomorrow night will understand something like that or will it need to be simpler?"

Then they ask *me* questions:

"How does your Braille watch work?" Then I open the crystal and feel the dots and they say, "I never thought of that."

"How do you get around so well? How can you travel all by yourself? How do you read music in

127

Braille?" And I explain for the hundred-thousandth time and try to sound as interested as if I were explaining it for the first time.

Tomorrow we'll run again—at the Bible college in the morning, lunch at noon, a short rest in the afternoon, dinner with the Joneses and an evening concert.

When the concert's over, back to the motel. A *long* conversation this time. He never came out of the woodwork until tonight and I never would have noticed him except he said pleadingly, "I want to talk to you." I knew there was a need there so we talked.

"I've been a Christian for three years and it never seems to work. I mean, I go to church and I've walked the aisles but I don't feel anything. I'm not happy. I have no power in my life."

"What did you expect?" I asked.

"Well, I thought things would be better and I thought I would be happy."

"Maybe you expected too much."

"Well, what good is being a Christian if I can't expect things from the Lord?"

"Maybe because you expect the wrong things you don't get anything."

"Well, Ken, I've gotten something."

"Oh, what?"

"Uh, I don't know. I guess I know I'm doing what's right."

"Do you need more reward than that?"

"No, maybe not, but isn't there more?"

"Yes, there well may be, but you can't expect a great

128

deal of emotional high or emotional satisfaction. You can't expect it always to be easy. You can expect to have to obey in spite of great difficulty . . ."

He interrupts. "Wait a minute. I've got to tell you what I really came for. You see, it's this girl."

"Oh?"

"You see, she's married and I've seen her several times and . . ."

"Where does it stand now?"

"Well, we broke it off."

"Is she a Christian?"

"Yeah."

"How does she feel?"

"She's worried too, and feels bad."

"But you've broken it off now?"

"Yeah, we don't see each other any more."

"You're forgiven, you know. You're not guilty."

"Actually, I saw her last night."

"Uh huh, how did you feel?"

"Not good."

"Do you want to stop seeing her?"

"Yeah, I really would and I've prayed about it but I keep wanting to see her."

"Do you expect the Lord to grab you by a string like a puppet and pull you away?"

"I guess not."

"Then it's a matter of your will, isn't it?"

"Yeah, did you ever have problems like that?"

"I've had problems like that. Let me tell you about . . ." And we talk on and on and on and when I'm tired at one o'clock in the morning, he's not, and we talk for another hour. I've got five hours to sleep and I have to be up at 7:00 A.M. Catch a plane at 8:00 A.M.

My Not-At-Home world is a fascinating place. So many people come into my experience. So many people who hurt and who are hungry, and they think they're hungry for answers. Really what we discover together is that they're hungry for relationships.

I come into so many homes that are happy and so many homes that are hurting. I see people who cover their loneliness with all sorts of masks. Why some of them choose to reveal themselves to me, I will never know. Maybe I'm an easy person to talk to. I hope so.

In the air again.

One more day, my jolly, one more day. There's one more song to sing. One more chapter to write. A few more chords to play.

It won't be long until Not-At-Home becomes At Home, but right now let's finish the evening out.

11

~~~~~~~~~~~~~~~~~~~~~~~~ *Lead the Way*

Speaking of ending the evening, I remember one time when the stage crew and I did not quite agree on when a concert should end—a misinterpretation of signals, I suppose. Anyway, just before the last song when all was quiet and expectation was high, the curtain suddenly closed! Talk about feeling stupid! After a moment of embarrassed silence the audience began to applaud and when the curtain reopened for my post-concert bow I was madly running around behind the piano looking for someone on the stage crew to inform him I wasn't through yet. I realized the curtain was opening, turned toward the audience, ran smack into the edge of the piano, and in general made an utter fool of myself. Someone came up later and wanted to book the end of the show for a nightclub act!

You and I won't have to worry about a curtain closing, but we are coming to the end of the concert. You've been on this piano bench with me all night, listening to me talk about me, hurting with me, rejoicing with me, learning about me, laughing with me and at me and for me.

Now, what about you? I want to ask something of you. I want to ask you to sing the last song *with* me, for the last song is a song that we can sing together. The last song is a traveling song that we can sing as we travel down the road of life's uncertainties together. Listen to the words. I'll teach them to you if you're willing to learn:

> There's no way in the world
> I can be everything love means for me to be,
> But, as long as morning breaks another day,
> Lord, I'm Yours, I'll follow, lead the way.

Do you experience, like I do, the sense of frustration, the sense of confusion about your life? The sense that, "There is *no* place to go from here," or the sense that, "I really don't know what I'm doing."

Do you know what it's like to sit down at a table and have a hundred things in front of you and not know which one to pick up? Do you know what it's like to walk onto the street and come to an intersection and see four directions and not know which one to choose? Do you know what it's like to have tried and tried and tried again and to feel that you've gotten nowhere? Have you come to the recognition of your limitations and your weaknesses? Or, are you hiding behind the mask of competence? Do you want me to believe you can do anything that you set your mind to do? Do you want me to believe you have your life all together? Do

132

you want me to believe that by saying "Praise the Lord" and "Hallelujah" fifty times a day and by going to this Bible study and that prayer meeting you can live a victorious, successful, triumphant, happy, glorious life? Are you trying to convince me that you don't hurt, that you don't need relationship, that you're not afraid to give yourself in love?

Well, if you're hiding behind the competence mask then, try if you will to remove the mask at least a little and let me see a part of your face. If you're willing to come with me to the point of saying, "There's no way in the world," then, let's go on with the song.

> There's no way in the world
> I can be . . .

So much of your life focuses on "doing." "I want to do good." "I want to do right." "I want to *do* this for you." "I want to do well by my friends." "I want to do well financially."

What about "being"? What about the person you *are?* What about your interior? What's happening inside you? How much of life are you living? How much of experience are you dealing with? How much of the range of possible emotions have you explored? Do you want to *be* rather than just do?

> There's no way in the world
> I can be everything love means for me to be . . .

What about love and you? How do the two of you get along? Are you afraid of love? Are you afraid to trust someone and give yourself in love? Are you afraid to open those windows to your heart?

You've listened to me be as honest as I know how to be for ten chapters. Are you saying to yourself, "I couldn't be that honest"? Or perhaps you've come to the place where I am, the place of saying, "Yes, I am afraid of this or that. I realize my limitations, but I want very much to love. I want to dare to love."

Love makes great demands, you know. It's curious that love can be demanding and nondemanding at the same time, for we talk about acceptance as a part of love. "I accept you for who you are. I do not condemn you for what you have done. I do not refuse to relate to you no matter where you have been, no matter what your past. Yet, if I love you I cannot help expecting the best from you. I cannot help wanting you to be what God intended you to be. I cannot help desiring for you freedom, independence, joy, honesty, openness."

So, love is demanding while it is accepting. If you love me, your very presence in my life demands a response which I can either deny or give. If I give that response, the more I love you the more we will demand of each other.

It's the same way with my love for God. God loves me perfectly, unconditionally, acceptingly. God OKs me. God does not condemn me. But, the closer I come to him, the more I learn about him and come to love him, the more he demands of my life.

There's no way in this world

I can be everything love means for me to be,
But, as long as morning breaks another day . . .

I am not concerned at this moment about five years from now, or ten years or fifteen years. I'm not concerned about our ultimate destiny. I am not concerned about the steps you will take long after you read this book. I am concerned at *this* moment about one step, for there is only one step. Now, when I take that step there is one more step, and if today I can take some steps toward loving, toward following my Savior's lead, toward discovering abundant living, then the night will come and I can sleep. And when morning breaks the darkness I can awake to face that *one more day*, taking one more step after one more step toward God and toward you.

There's no way in this world
I can relive all the times I took and did
not give . . .

Yes, I freely admit mistakes and failures. I will always suffer from being the kind of kid who could lie easily. I will always suffer from having lost most of a sense of conscience during my early college years.

What about you? What do you suffer from? What in your past makes you ache? What skeletons are in your closet that you are afraid to show me? What are you trying to live down? What reputation have you gained that you don't want? What sins have you committed that you're afraid to talk about? What battle scars are on your body?

You cannot relive nor completely remove the sting and the hurt of the past, but again . . .

As long as morning breaks another . . .

Yes, that's it—another step. *Today* give me strength, Lord. *Today* let me live your way. *Today* let me lay aside the stigma, the sting, the anguish and the bitterness of the past.

> And it's no good to keep on crying over past
> mistakes,
> And it's no good to keep on worrying about
> unlucky breaks . . .

Speaking of unlucky breaks, I could say I had my share, could you? I wouldn't doubt you could. As we sit here together finishing our last song, you could probably tell me about numerous times and situations where you've been gyped, jilted, hurt, passed by. But, that's gone, too, isn't it? *Today* is what's left to us. *Today* and tomorrow will be a *today* when it gets here.

Are you still living with the memory of your unlucky breaks? Are you still feeding off those experiences that can do nothing but poison your mind?

> And it's no use to keep on trying
> to fix up yesterday . . .

There are things I can't change now. There are marks on the books that can't be erased. I cannot *un*hurt the people I have hurt. A thousand apologies will not take

136

away the scars that my life has placed on someone else's. You cannot change, either, what you have done. If you have hurt someone, if you have made mistakes that have caused unpleasantness, unhappiness, business failure, bankruptcy, loss of family—those things are gone. They cannot be changed.

What is left is an opportunity for new life.

> The day is here, there's life to live,
>   It's time to grow,
> I dare not throw it away.

Do you spend so much time wishing you could correct yesterday or wishing you could be what you are not, that you lose precious moments you could be living *now?* Do you find that hours go by and you've been so preoccupied with the "has beens" and the "used to bes" and the "ought to bes" that you've forgotten to live and to celebrate?

> There's no way in this world
> I can do everything love means for me to do . . .

So stop striving compulsively. Stop running around on your treadmill. Stop accepting every job that comes to you because you're trying to impress or trying to make yourself better. Stop running yourself into the ground in our fast-paced ulcerated life for that kind of *doing* will not help you.

When you feel you have not done what love demands and when you feel the need to rush out and reach out, stop a moment. Recognize who you are. You're not the captain of the team. Let all of your *doing* come out of your *being*.

> There's no way in the world
> I can do everything love means for me to do,
> But as long as morning breaks another day,
> [and here's the key]
> Lord, I'm Yours, I'll follow, lead the way.

Can you sing that song with me? Are you willing to walk into the uncertainties of a Christian life that does not depend on easy answers? that does not depend on doctrines and propositions? that does not depend on "having it all together"? Are you willing to join me on my journey into relationships? Are you willing to take the hand of the Master and let him lead you down a road you do not know?

I'd like for us to go together. I'd like to count you as one of my fellow travelers because I'll *need* you. I'll need to depend on you sometimes when I get tired and you'll need to depend on me, too. We'll need to hang on tightly to each other when the wind blows and floods come up around our feet. Sometimes I won't be able to see him except through you. Are you willing to go?

Let's get up now. The concert's over, and I've gained a new friend. We close the piano and walk off the stage. Soon I'll board a plane and the roar of jet engines and the smell of coffee in the galley will let me know I'm going home—and that's a good place to go!

A Personal Note

I watched Ken Medema perform before thousands of people in symphony hall at the Atlanta Memorial Arts Center in Atlanta, Georgia, one Saturday night in September of 1975. I was amazed at his ability to hold an audience so rapt. Most had not heard his music before and this was the night of an unforgettable first.

The following morning (after driving through a "rainy night in Georgia" while Ken talked sleepily into a tape recorder) I watched Ken sit down at a piano in First Baptist Church of Augusta, Georgia, and improvise a song taken from Scripture read by the pastor.

That evening this phenomenal music man gave a full concert for First Baptist and one question to me on the drive to the church was, "Joyce, what should I play and sing tonight?" Before I could answer Ken said, "That's OK, I'll just let the Holy Spirit lead."

My, and did the Spirit have free rein in that concert! I knew this man was physically drained and it's common knowledge his mind runs (never walks) constantly from one idea to another. And yet, because of Ken's unique personality and kaleidoscopic makeup, that night he really let go and let God!

On another occasion I sat in a very small church on the outskirts of Big Spring, Texas, and watched him give a forty-five-minute concert to a congregation of approximately twenty-five (that included children). It's more than obvious that Ken believes "where two or more are gathered, there I am . . ." for he never measures the quality of a concert by the number of seats filled.

He gave two more concerts that Sunday, and on Monday gave two more. Tuesday morning bright and early we drove to the Dallas/Ft. Worth airport where Ken caught a plane for Kansas City. He had an evening's performance there.

He flew out of Kansas City immediately following that concert, and because of a layover in Chicago arrived in Newark airport as the sun was coming up Wednesday. This is a typical, long Ken Medema weekend.

Now, I consider myself in fairly good physical condition. I've stomped for eight weeks all over Europe. I guided thirty people on a tour of the Middle East and I play (and sometimes win) a pretty good game of touch football with my eight-year-old godson, Jonathon Erik.

However, keeping up with Kenneth Peter Medema is like being water boy for every participant in the Olympics. His energies seem supernatural and as many times as I traveled with him to work on this book, I must admit now, before Ken and the rest of the world— I never got used to that cheery, enthusiastic voice on the other end of a 6 A.M. wake-up call.

"Good morning, Joyce. It's a delicious morning and I'm ravishingly hungry. I'll meet you outside your door in twenty minutes. I'm dying for a cheese omelette, sausage, coffee . . ."

Working with Ken on this book has made me look at my life as a Christian and as a human being from many new angles. He's posed challenges, asked questions, shared his views of certain Scripture with me, prayed with me and for me. Together, we've prayed with waitresses, managers and fellow residents in motels where we've stayed. Ken simply (and it *is* simple for him) walks around smiling, loving and giving.

Although blind, Ken improved my heart vision by many degrees. From a man who cannot see, I was helped to see things I'd missed before I met him. Words like *sensitivity*, *aching*, *weeping*, *touching*, *caring*, *reaching* all weigh more now than before I spent time with him.

To watch him sit with tape recorder in hand and talk five chapters one right after the other into the machine with perhaps three stops to repeat a sentence I was amazed! His memory is something no writer would attempt to explore on paper.

Time spent with Ken, his warm, loving parents in Michigan, his beautiful wife and the son he's so justly proud of—all have added new dimensions to my life and each one showed me more of the Jesus Ken sings so vibrantly of.

If you enjoyed reading this book just half as much as I enjoyed working with Ken on it, then you really like it a lot! It's seldom, after a writer has typed for twelve hours straight, that the rereading of a certain chapter brings tears because the words are so real, so honest and so full of the power of the Holy Spirit. I believe that's a compliment, Ken. I've read it many times and although I typed every word, I'm still underlining in my own book!

I wish to thank Ken Medema, my brother in Christ, for sharing so much of his Jesus with me. I thank him, also, for taking me on flying adventures either with a song or one of his inimitable original stories and not only letting me see a larger, more sufficient God, but helping me hear the laughter of God, as well.

Thank you, Ken, for letting me "roam the Father's land" with you for awhile. I shall never forget it. And now, because of this book, I can say with so much more definiteness and meaning:

"Lord, I'm yours, I'll follow, lead the way."

JOYCE NORMAN